BEYOND LIMITATIONS

From a boy without promise to the man I am today

BEYOND
LIMITATIONS

*From a boy
without promise
to the man
I am today*

Marc Williams

Printed in the United States of America

Published by MarcWilliamsSpeaks

www.MarcWilliamsSpeaks.com

ISBN 978-0-9903802-0-7

Library of Congress Control Number: 2014908952

Cover Design by Elizabeth Van Itallie

Logo Design by John Glozek

CONTENT

Acknowledgements

After speaking at a Martial Arts school, I mentioned that I was writing a book. And the first question was, "When will it be available?" I vowed on that day that by the end of the following summer, the book would be published. The truth is I had already started working on this book over a year prior to that speaking engagement, but I had not made a definitive commitment to finish it by a particular deadline. Once I committed to it, I finished it, or at least I finished the complete first draft. I still consider that the most difficult achievement in the process. And now what you have in your hands is the final, most satisfying achievement in the process, the final product. But I would be remiss if I shared my words with the world without acknowledging those who have supported me and helped me to transfer my thoughts to paper. Thank you to my wife Lauren for your love, your support, and your endless encouragement. Thank you to Jackie and Sonia for reading the book before anyone else. I treasure your time, feedback, and suggestions. Thank you to my friends in the English Department at Brooklyn Tech for your support. Thank you to Tim for your advice about the book title. Thank you to Trish, Rich, and Phyllis for your help and guidance with the cover of the book; that's probably where I needed the greatest help. And thank you to Danny for introducing me to Elizabeth who designed the cover. Thank you to Marni for putting me in touch with Mark who gave me some good advice about publishing. Thank you to Lou, Scott, and my family of friends who I affectionately call "the fellas" for always having my back. Thank you to my fellow Toastmasters for your support and encouragement. Thank you to my family…we don't talk as much as I know we should, but your love is eternal and it is because of you that I am who I've become. And finally, thank you to Jordan, Sydney, and Dylan, my three children….though it may seem like you played no role in putting this whole thing together, you are the reasons why I do everything I do…you are my motivation!

Introduction: In Loving Memory
My Mother's Gift

On Christmas Day, 2010, before I ever woke up to open presents for my mother's grandchildren, Jordan and Sydney, I saw my mother. It was my greatest Christmas gift. I saw my mother in my dreams. I don't even remember the context of the dream. I just remember waking up later and being happy. My mother, Johanna Williams, passed away during the summer of 1996. That was the worst day of my life. I may never recover from that day, but I will always forever be grateful to my mommy. Her struggle and her obstacles are memorialized through the success that I have experienced. Success: that's a relative term. I think I'm successful in many ways (after all, I am the son of an illiterate mother, a son who eventually became the Assistant Principal of English at one of the most prestigious high schools in the entire United States; and that's not irony; that's success, my success; my mother's success, our success), but I also think that I have a long way to go. And that's not an indication of dissatisfaction or unhappiness. It's an indication of a hunger. I'm hungry! And I want you to be hungry too!

Let's be honest: we all want something more out of life. We all want to be successful. We all want to find a way to endure the struggle and achieve the success we so desire. And the hardest part of the climb is all the obstacles that stand in our way. Diane Westlake once said, "Whatever the struggle, continue the climb. It may be only one step to the summit." But I'm sure I speak for many of you who feel that you've had your fair share and more than enough of the obstacles. Now you want the success. Now you want the answers. Now you want the plan. Well, on my journey, I have found, through my endeavors as a teacher, that sharing my struggles and the principles that have taken me from a kid without promise to a man with potential may be helpful to other people…it may be helpful to you.

When I first sat down to write this book, it was December 28th, my mother's birthday. So I want to say, "Thank you mommy. Thank you for continuing to be my inspiration to better myself and hopefully to help others to embrace their struggles, discover their motivation, develop their potential, and achieve their success."

Chapter One: Elevate Your Mind

"A true man is one who overcomes the ups and downs of life with fortitude. One should not recoil before reverses of fortunes. One should bravely face them and overcome them." - Sri Sathya Sai Baba

Minutes after I spoke to a group of foster children about the importance of being positive and strategies for fostering positive relationships, one young man sat next to me and told me his story. Like me, he is a self-proclaimed "momma's boy". No one meant any more to him than his mother. She was everything to him. And so he will never forget the night the paramedics rushed into his home. He thought the alarm was about one of his small cousins who lived in the house. But as he stepped out into the hall, he saw his mother gasping for air. The paramedics were struggling to lay her quivering body on the stretcher. He watched the red lights fade away into the curtains of a cold rain. For days, he stood by the side of her hospital bed. And when the doctors needed to be alone with her, he only stepped as far as the entrance of the room, standing watch. The doctor's final word makes him cry every day. His life was never the same.

His father took him in, but they lived in a room in a building where they shared the kitchen and the bathroom with other people. His father only had two pairs of keys, one for himself and one for his girlfriend, but none for his son. Every day, his son would return home from school, only to wait hours before his father would finally wake up to let him in. That problem was easily resolved for the next nine months: his father just kept him out of school.

Shortly afterwards, they found themselves living in a shelter, living the same lifestyle his mother vowed he would never live again. Eventually, his father was able to rent two rooms, blocks away from each other. He and his girlfriend lived in one room. His son lived alone in the other room, still without a key. For eight days, no one came to see if he was ok. And he couldn't leave the house because no one was there to let him back in. He was without food. He was without electricity. He was without care. All he had was running water. He said that he took showers several times a day just because it was the only way to make the time pass. On the ninth day, he searched through a bag his father had left in the apartment. He found two things: a gold ring and a "Cash for Gold" business card. He took his chances and left his room, the door unlocked. But when he approached the "Cash for Gold" window, he was told that the ring was not real gold. Distraught, he found himself begging for money that night, just to make a phone call. He called his aunt, only to hear voices in the background, but no one said a word. The click of the phone, followed by the buzz of a busy signal left him distraught, left him hopeless. Days later, he found himself in foster care. When I met him that day, he was close to aging out of foster care, with no new family to call his own.

Life can be so unfair sometimes.

I asked him what his plans are. He said he plans to go into the military. He refuses to do anything counterproductive because he made a promise to his mother.

I told him to reach out to me any time he wants to talk. He never called, but I can only hope that by our paths crossing, that he reignited his passion to rise beyond that which has held him down.

When we are struggling…when we are feeling defeated and hopeless, we need to be resurrected and re-energized. Sometimes, we need someone else to help us dig deeper so that we can find the drive within ourselves to match the desire and the potential that exists within us. I've been lucky enough to have people in my life to lift me, from family to friends, from teachers to mentors. Some of you know whom these people are in your lives, those who can lift you when you feel all hope is lost. Some of you may think you have no one else. But know this, these people do exist in your life. If not at home, they are at your school, at your job, in your church, in your community center, in that book, or on that podcast. We may see them everyday, but we may never notice the power they possess. *The nurse who lived across the hall from my mother and I will never know the positive role she and her son played in my life. I may have made eye contact with her twice. I may have said hello to her son once. She worked late nights to make ends meet. And her son, a latchkey kid, never got into trouble. I didn't realize it at the time, but as I reflect on it today, I was inspired by them to work hard. And when I saw them move out of my neighborhood, I was inspired to believe that one day I could move too. They were our neighbors, but we didn't really know them. But we knew they existed.* These people exist in our lives. And we don't even need to know them personally; we just have to know that they exist; we need to see what they do, and we need to listen to how they communicate to themselves and with others.

But I'd be remiss if I didn't admit that some people, myself included, also have something within us: an inner strength, a natural ability to motivate ourselves. I have yet to figure out how to bottle that and sell it as an energy drink, but through some reflection, I have identified the habits that have kept me motivated, even at times when I, like everybody else, find myself struggling against moments of discouragement and frustration. And I'm glad that I've had the opportunity to reflect on my experiences because I believe that we cannot allow the feelings of discouragement to allow moments of defeat. When we feel like we are falling from grace, we need to be lifted onto our feet again.

I learned recently that reading words of encouragement, reading words of prayer, sitting in natural sunlight, giving someone a hug, breathing deeply with your eyes closed, listening to your favorite tune, or eating foods high in Vitamin D are just a few proven strategies that we can use to naturally lift our spirits. Try one of them…and then come back in a few minutes, and continue reading…

****

"Hope rises like a phoenix from the ashes of shattered dreams."
-S.A. Sachs

Weeks before speaking to a group of disenfranchised unemployed and underemployed adults, I read this story…A woman had been unemployed for four years. After searching for jobs with no success for ten months she thought she would go back to school and obtain her associates degree, hoping that it would help. While doing this, she kept applying for jobs, doing whatever she thought she was qualified to do.

4

BEYOND LIMITATIONS

She had several interviews, but nothing came of them. She volunteered for a 30-day job with possible employment at the end of the period, but after 30 days, she was not hired. She continued to apply for jobs, but only had a few interviews. Her unemployment ran out at the end of the summer. She had just enough saved to pay rent through the fall. She and her roommate scrambled, because she didn't have an income and was unable to pay her portion of the rent. She expected to be homeless in a few weeks.

Life can be so unfair sometimes.

But where there is despair, we must dig deeper to find the hope and the answers that lie below the surface. If we never give up, then we will eventually find a way. So here's what I said to that room full of disenfranchised people, who walked into a room looking for hope...

"You are going to find what you need and what you want. And the most important thing you need to do to make that happen is exercise your mind and use the power of your mentality. Because within our brains lies the power; and with this power, we can overcome any struggle; we can turn any struggle from a source of frustration into a source of inspiration because if we can get through anything then we can do anything. Remember, struggle is only temporary; but the possibility to do anything we want is endless.

After doing some research about the current state of unemployment in our country, I learned that 14 million people are unemployed. And out of that 14 million, 4.5 million of them have been unemployed for over a year. 1 million of them would take any job they can get, but have to go back to school or take care of a sick family member. And 800,000 of them are so frustrated that they have given up looking for a job and are relying on what they have left in their savings and finding the few opportunities to make a little bit of money off the books. So what's the difference between the 800,000 and the other 13 million: Motivation, Positivity, Mentality!"

I received an email shortly after I spoke that day. I was informed that six of the people in that group were offered jobs that same day.

That proves it.

Life can get better.

*"The experienced mountain climber is not intimidated by a mountain --
he is inspired by it. The persistent winner is not discouraged by a
problem -- he is challenged by it. Mountains are created to be
conquered; adversities are designed to be defeated; problems are sent to
be solved." –William Arthur Ward*

After sixteen years of teaching some of the best students and
serving some of the greatest parents, I have discovered that there is also a
great need to motivate our youth. The statistics concerning drop out rates,
college readiness, and professional success are staggering. The stories
about crimes, substance abuse, and overall apathy are frightening.

*In an article published by PubMed and the U.S. National Library
of Science, clinical pediatrician GB Landman stated a "lack of motivation
was seen as the primary cause of school difficulties in 80 children
(49%)."*

*According to the Parent Corner at Broadalbin-Perth Central
School, "Research indicates that many teens have become apathetic
toward things that they should consider important. This indifference often
leads to unfinished homework, missed practices, or poor school
attendance. Although apathy in high school is an age-old problem, the
stakes are higher in this highly competitive world. Understanding the
roots of apathy and learning to help teens find a clear focus, maintain a
positive attitude, and develop good study habits can improve the chances
that those students will ultimately succeed in high school and beyond."*

But it's not only indifference that holds them back. There are other
challenges:

BEYOND LIMITATIONS

Instant Gratification: Young people can get just about anything these days in an instant and with very little effort. As a result, hard work, perseverance, and dedication have lost their value. They don't have to go to the store to buy a book; they have kindles. They don't have to go to the library to do research; they have Google. They don't have to write a research paper; they can pay a fee and download one. Instant gratification may be the downfall of self-motivation.

Reluctant Role Models: I used to shy away from that label, but then I realized how important a responsibility it is. We are all role models, whether we want to be or not, because Imitation is a Natural Instinct. Have you ever heard a toddler repeat a curse word? Have you heard people suggest that the best way to potty train a child is through demonstration? Have you ever heard an adult tell a kid, "Do what I say, not what I do", only to hear the kid respond, "But you did it!"? Impressions are unavoidable, but if we say that we are not motivated to lead by example, then our kids will have no example by which to follow and succeed and, in turn, will not be motivated to succeed, nor motivated to lead.

Acceptance: I'm guilty of saying it, but the statement "It is what it is" is a tragic code to live by. When young people accept that "that's just the way it is" they may not be motivated to face their challenges or overcome their obstacles. And just as bad, when adults accept that young people are unmotivated "because that's just the way kids are these days", then that becomes a self-fulfilling prophecy. Non-acceptance may be the fuel for motivation.

So I'm also writing this book for every kid who struggles with what he knows he needs to do, but just can't or won't do it…not yet. I want to help them. And I believe that I can.

According to Dr. Jim Taylor, author of Positive Pushing: How to Raise a Successful and Happy Child, "Though we cannot change the biological and psychological factors impacting children's behavior, we can teach the unmotivated to be motivated and the irresponsible to be responsible."

I'm also writing this book for those young hopefuls who have pushed themselves to early success only to find that their futures after college seem grim.

I read an article called *"Chasing the American Dream: Recent College Graduates and the Great Recession," published by Rutgers University in 2012* that stated, *"many college graduates who graduated during the past several years are facing historic obstacles in achieving the foundations of the American dream and express low expectations for their future prosperity...More than one in four are living with their parents or family members to save money, and significant numbers of recent college graduates are delaying major purchases, putting off their graduate education, taking extra jobs to supplement their income, and even delaying marriage...The cream of the crop of America's youth, graduates of four-year colleges and universities, believe that the American dream of upward mobility may have stopped with them...Young, well-educated people, who are typically optimistic about their futures, are expressing doubt in another cornerstone of the American dream."*

It's hard to be optimistic given these circumstances, isn't it? And yet, Heller Keller once said...

"Optimism is the faith that leads to achievement. Nothing can be done without hope and confidence." - Anonymous

To rise beyond the obstacles we face, we need optimism, guidance, and motivation. And the truth is, regardless of age, race, religion, background, experience, economic status, gender, or any other distinction, we all have and will face struggles from which we need to find the strength to endure and overcome. So I'm writing this book for anyone who may find some inspiration in my words...

BEYOND LIMITATIONS

The Ashes that Burn the Soles of his Feet Will be the Light that Will Lead Us Beyond the Fire.

"Believe that there's light at the end of the tunnel. Believe that you might be that light for someone else." -Kobi Yamada

I'm writing this book for the hopeful homeowners without the home, the thousands of hard workers without a job, the aspiring entrepreneurs without the customers, the artists without the audience or even the audition, the athletes without a team or even a tryout, the students without the marks, the graduates without the prospects, the parents who just don't know what else to do, the patients without a miracle, and the people who seem to only have a prayer and promise to fulfill, who are looking for the strength to fight and the will to win...

We Will Win!

I hope that I can give you that boost, one that will reenergize and charge you, one that will inspire you to push yourself beyond your limits and past your struggles to realize what you can really do, one that will motivate you to maximize your potential to do anything you want, and one that will supply you with the mindset you need to Rise Beyond!

I hope this book will be like that movie you watch that fires you up and makes you want to take on the world...because you just witnessed the story of a person, real or not, who faced the unbelievable, who was nearly broken but found a way, and crawled his way out of a hole until he stood tall.

I hope this book will be like the music you play in your headphones when you're on the treadmill or running that last lap, exhausted, struggling for the strength to last one more minute, to make it through that one last incline.

I hope this book will be the voice inside your head that refuses to quit; that refuses to believe that it cannot be done; the voice that motivates you.

BEYOND LIMITATIONS

That's what I want, but I must confess...I don't profess to have the answers to every problem. Hell, I still have my own problems, obstacles, and challenges that I am fighting to overcome. But what I can give you is what has and continues to drive me...what has and continues to work for me...a piece of my mind. The mind is an incredible tool. Research, that dates back to 1890 when William James discovered what scientists now call neuroplasticity, shows that we have the ability to rewire our brains, to change the structure and the function of our brains, to strengthen the prefrontal cortex of our brains. And the result is that we can stimulate positive feelings that control our emotions and behaviors, which helps us to focus on the goals we want to achieve. Yes, we need actions to achieve our goals, but if actions were so easy, we'd all be where we want to be right now. Actions need to be driven. Our minds are positioned at the steering wheel. Knowing that means that I will never stop driving until I get to where I want to go. So ride with me. And when the journey gets tough and you feel like you just want to stop because you feel like you're driving in circles or you feel like you've crashed into that wall one too many times, or you feel like you just don't have enough in your pocket to put more gas in the tank...pick up this book, and just read another page. Just read another page, not because I'm some guru of positivity, not because I have some secret to the stars, not because of anything to do with me....just read another page, because deep down inside, everyone wants to win in the end....just read another page, because you want to win in the end.

Motivation is the fuel in our tank.

But it burns, like any other fuel.

So we just need to refuel it.

So we can move forward.

BEYOND LIMITATIONS

What keeps me going is the belief that I can fly.

"If I can see it, then I can do it
If I just believe it, there's nothing to it
I believe I can fly
I believe I can touch the sky
I think about it every night and day
Spread my wings and fly away
I believe I can soar
I see me running through that open door
I believe I can fly

I believe I can fly."

R. Kelly sang the words that remind me of my late aunt Grace. She loved that song. I love that song too. It keeps me going.

Everything in my life points to the fact that I should have stopped by now. Everything in my life points to the fact that I should have been another statistic. I was a young black male, growing up in a poor, black neighborhood. I was exposed to violence and death. My mother was illiterate. My mother was single. And though she had a boyfriend who lived with us for nearly ten years, he was an alcoholic. He was unemployed. He had a prison record. Our only sources of income were welfare checks, food stamps, and a Medicaid card. I could have been another statistic, but that didn't happen. I could have become frustrated, defeated, demoralized, but that didn't happen. I became the exception to the rule. And now I aim to make the exception the rule.

I learned at a very young age how to harness the power of aspiration, self-motivation, positivity, discipline, and hard work.

(Aspiration): "I have discovered in life that there are ways of getting almost anywhere you want to go, if you really want to go."
-Langston Hughes

11

BEYOND LIMITATIONS

(Self-Motivation): *"You are essentially who you create yourself to be and all that occurs in your life is the result of your own making."*
-Stephen Richards

(Positivity): *"Keep your thoughts positive because your thoughts become your words. Keep your words positive because your words become your behavior. Keep your behavior positive because your behavior becomes your habits. Keep your habits positive because your habits become your values. Keep your values positive because your values become your destiny."* **-Mahatma Gandhi**

(Discipline): *"No horse gets anywhere until he is harnessed. No stream or gas drives anything until it is confined. No Niagara is ever turned into light and power until it is tunneled. No life ever grows great until it is focused, dedicated, disciplined."* **-Harry Emerson Fosdick**

(Hard Work): *"If your dream is a big dream, and if you want your life to work on the high level that you say you do, there's no way around doing the work it takes to get you there."* **-Joyce Chapman**

After listening to so many people ask me, "What keeps you going?" and "Why are you always so positive?", I stepped back and reflected on my life...my story. And I started to remember the moments and words that continue to push me to this day. And I want to share those moments and words with you...with someone....with anyone....just for the chance that maybe...just maybe...it will resonate with you and help you Rise Beyond....

We all have aspirations. We all have struggles too. And so we all need some motivation in our lives. So consider this my contribution to the pursuit of your aspirations.

Enjoy!

Chapter Two: Embrace Your Struggle

"If you are distressed by anything external, the pain is not due to the thing itself, but to your estimate of it; and this you have the power to revoke at any moment." -Marcus Aurelius

I believe that we have the mental capacity to render any pain or any fear powerless, but I also believe that...

Fear is a Tool We Can Use to Take Flight.

So be afraid of the life that you do not want to live.

Be motivated by a fear of what you don't want out of life,

So that you can be driven to pursue the life that you desire.

I talk a lot about role models and mentors. It all reminds me of that age-old question, "Who has had the greatest influence in your life?" Who motivates you? Who inspires you? Upon reflection, it's often not who influenced me, but rather what influences me. One of my greatest motivations has been emerging, not escaping, but emerging from a lifestyle I was so afraid of when I was young.

Fear: I feared for my life sometimes.

I will never forget the night I returned home after a work night at Urban Outfitters. I worked in the Village in New York City. But I lived in the Pink Houses in East New York, Brooklyn. It was an hour ride on the subway. I took the A-train to the last stop in Brooklyn: Grant Avenue. The walk from the train station to my 2726 Linden Blvd building in the projects was not a short distance. I walked that dark, desolate street every night, alone. At midnight, it was scary. My closest friend's father was stabbed on that block. I'm sure that countless other assaults happened on that block. I couldn't have walked any faster than I did on those late nights. I walked under the elevated ramp to be out of sight. I wore my headphones slightly off my ear so that I could be alert and at the same time, so that I could have something to distract me from the fear. When I finally reached Linden Boulevard, I felt a sense of relief. I was almost home.

One particular night, I walked through the back door of my apartment building. The front of the building had better lighting, but it also had the regulars standing outside on the front stoop. I just didn't want to walk pass them. Many of them I knew from growing up in the neighborhood, like the boy whose most hurtful prank was placing a lit cigarette butt in the elastic of my underwear.

I sat on the stoop one day just listening to the other kids talk about things that went in one ear and out the other. Feeling like I didn't belong, I craved to be a part of that circle. And as I daydreamed through whatever it was that they were talking about, I felt a sting along the skin of my lower back. I leaped into the air to the shattering of their laughter. Years later, these were the same boys standing outside on the front stoop.

Maybe there was nothing to fear that night, but my instincts kept me from going through the front of the building. Sometimes, after walking through the back entrance, if I peeked and saw any of those boys hanging out by the front stoop, I'd run up to the second floor to call the elevator. My heart raced. Getting to the 8th floor brought me closer to relief, but not quite. I fumbled through the keys, opened the door, and locked it quickly behind me.

"Hi mommy!"

BEYOND LIMITATIONS

Watching her lean over to glance at me, as she lay in her room in the dark, the glare of the light off the TV screen making her face barely visible was my reassurance that she was okay. The money from the job helped a lot. But leaving my mother home alone for hours was unsettling.

That same night, hours after eating a cold meal my mother left on the stove for me, hours past turning off the television to go to sleep, there was a knock at the door. I was so scared. I crept to the door, slowing moving the peephole, hoping that whoever was on the other side of the door could not sense that I was there.

Flashbacks of that little boy hiding underneath the pillows of his mother's couch crept in my mind and overshadowed my thoughts.

My heart raced. But my mind was confused and relieved at the same time. It was the sight of two police officers. Apparently there was a shooting in the back of my building that night. Seemingly, it happened shortly after I had gotten home. To this day, I am thankful that I made it home minutes earlier. I could have been that victim. I could have died that night. Each night I walked home, I was afraid I would die.

The same was true years earlier when I would work for Youth Patrol. One of my closest friends is always amused by my "war stories" of my time with "Youth on the Move". But at the time, it was a far cry from amusing. It was an after school job in the Cypress Hills Projects. My cousin told me about the job. He found a way to make some money legitimately. I couldn't turn down the opportunity for a paycheck.

I value a dollar and I want my kids to have those same values, but I would not want them to experience what I had to experience just to have a few extra bucks.

So it was Halloween night. The seven of us patrolled the neighborhood. And as we walked along the grass, we heard the battle cry, "Youth on the Move". Suddenly, rocks darted passed our heads.

BEYOND LIMITATIONS

"Run!!!!"

I thought I fractured my thumb as I slipped on the staircase, running for my life to reach the roof. And there we stood on the rooftop, crying into the walkie-talkie for Mr. Billups, our adult supervisor, to come and rescue us. Shamefully, we followed him out of the building, listening to the neighborhood kids scatter in laughter.

Then there was the late Thursday night when we entered one building to check the staircase and hallways for broken lights. But we were distracted this time. On the elevator ride upstairs, all we could think about was what we would do when it was time to walk out of the building. We were pretty certain that the threat was serious. Of the seven of us, there was one girl in our group. And before we had ever stepped into that building, two other girls from the neighborhood had laced her with several unspeakable names and promised to "jump" her the minute she came back outside. And when we stepped outside, that's exactly what happened. And as much as we wanted to help her, a gang of boys stood before us, barricaded us, out-numbered us, dared us. So we watched. Her hair was pulled. Her clothes were torn. Her body was bruised. Her face was scarred. She never went back to Youth Patrol. And I never told my mother, never told Sonny, and I never told Aunt Grace.

I never told them about many of the nights similar to that one. I never told them how I would walk in the center of the four lanes of Linden Boulevard on my way home at 10pm. I walked in the center, prepared to run either way just in case I saw any group of kids who could sense and prey upon my fears. I was happy when I finally got my ten-speed bike. I learned to pedal with great speed, because I knew of many kids who were tossed from their bikes, never to see those bikes again, but without fail to see the kids who took those bikes and acted like they had never seen you before.

I never told...because I didn't want to have to give up the job. It felt good to have a paycheck, even if it was only $50 for two weeks of work. It was nothing, but it was more than I had. And I learned very early how to stretch a dollar for an extended amount of time.

16

BEYOND LIMITATIONS

So I never told my mother about anything that happened, except when I had no choice, because of what happened in broad daylight. While on patrol, I heard a kid I have never seen before whisper, that I was this kid he knew. Now I knew whom he was talking about, but he definitely had the wrong guy. But it didn't matter as he and his friends followed us, screaming threats about what he was going to do to me. And as I stopped in front of the door of someone's house, three or four boys kicked and stomped me to the floor. The other guys on Youth Patrol just stood there and watched; they were just as frozen as the night that girl was jumped. They told me later that they were too afraid to do anything because they went to school with those boys. So they watched; they watched as the boots pounded me up against an apartment door. The door swung open fiercely as a woman with the voice of a bullhorn scared them off. She thought we were all just goofing around. But I had nothing to laugh about. That night I told Aunt Grace the story, and she begged me to quit. She promised to give me an allowance. But I didn't quit, not until the next time...

Working in a retail store in the Village, during my college years, was much safer, more enjoyable, and much more profitable. It only lost its luster after I clocked out and began the trip back to my neighborhood. But I still went to work each night. I still walked that long, dimly lit street each night. I still slipped through the back door of the building. I still called my mother between classes, during my 30 minute breaks at work, and before I stepped down into the subway to come home....I still kept my pocket full of quarters for the countless times I used a payphone to call my mother throughout the day to check to make sure she was okay...because thoughts of her sitting in her room alone, vulnerable, gave me chills. Feeling that I had to tell my mother not to answer the phone unless she heard my voice or Aunt Grace's voice or Aunt Niameh's voice on the answering machine was disheartening.

But I refused to let that fear defeat me.

I knew that I was working hard towards something...towards getting us out of the projects. I so desperately wanted to get us out of a life where we didn't have to live in fear. If we were going to emerge, it would have to be up to me. And as powerless as fear often made me feel, I used that fear to empower me, to motivate me.

Weeks after Dwayne Wade won his third NBA title, he received the "Humanitarian of the Year Award" because of his charitable work for the youth in his hometown of Chicago. During his acceptance speech, he talked about his memories of watching drug wars and gun violence right outside his window. And he vowed as a small child that the "windows of his world" would not be a "mirror of his future". He would emerge and do something different with his life, something better for him and for his family.

He used fear as a tool to take flight.

Fear is a powerful weapon. It has the power to defeat our minds…but only if we let it.

I read an article titled "How Fear Affects the Brain" by Carl Zimmer that was printed in Discover Magazine in 2010 that stated that *"fear powers up a forebrain network. That network sharpens the brain's attention to the things that threaten us, evaluates that threat, and runs through possible responses. The forebrain then keeps the midbrain shutdown to prevent us from acting impulsively, and possibly irrationally. In other words, the forebrain helps us to stay calm so we can assess the situation and make a decision that best serves us. However, studies show that while afraid, our forebrain's grip on the midbrain loosens, causing us to imagine threats that do not exist and seeing things as far more imminent than they really are."*

If we allow ourselves to do it, we can escalate our fears and strengthen negative thoughts…but only if we allow ourselves to do it. When we become aware of how our brains operate and how much power we wield over our brains, we will not be the deer frozen in headlights, stuck in a situation we don't desire, stuck in a situation we fear. Instead, we can empower ourselves mentally, think positively, and motivate ourselves to emerge. As Robert Wilson wrote in his article "The Most Powerful Motivator", fear is a powerful motivator when we have a solution, or "a new path to follow." There is always a new path to follow.

BEYOND LIMITATIONS

There is always a way out. I used to say that to myself all the time…there must be a way out. And now, I think about that all the time. Whatever I do, I can't go back. I refuse to go back…because I'm afraid to go back. I don't ever want that life for myself again and I most definitely don't want that life for my family.

I choose to use fear not as a decision between fight or flight, but rather as a driving force to fight so that I can fly.

But it wasn't only the fear for my life, or my mother's life that haunted me. I had other fears as well…fears that still haunt me to this day.

I remember as a kid, I was fully aware that I was poor. I told myself recently that while my kids are too young to be aware of such a thing now, that when they are old enough, I don't want them to know what it's like to be poor. I don't want Jordan, Sydney, or Dylan to stand in a store as I did, huddled over the cookie rack, staring at a fifty-cent pack of cookies, reluctant to ask, because I was fully aware that I could not to ask my mother to buy me a pack of fifty-cent cookies. I just knew we couldn't afford it.

Growing up poor was humbling.

Sometimes, I'd take a piece of gum and chew it for hours to make it last. I actually think it's because of all that gum chewing that I developed TMJ. After I chewed all the sugar out of the gum, I'd go to the kitchen and pull up the sugar bowl so that I could sprinkle a little more on the gum. Sugar was a gateway from reality. It sweetened many bowls of cornflakes in water, when we didn't have the milk. It was the one thing we somehow never ran out of, even though neighbors would knock at the door to ask if they could borrow some sugar.

Nevertheless we were poor, and I'm afraid to live a life like that again.

I'm afraid to revisit being that kid in middle school, going to a school outside of my district, a district full of kids who knew little if anything about being on welfare. After hanging out with school friends who would later walk to their high-rise apartment buildings, blocks away from the school, I began my walk home, miles away. Watching the city buses drive by multiple times was humbling. And it was a very lonely walk. For most of the walk, there was no one to walk by. I'd walk pass the Boulevard Housing Projects, pass the ASPCA, pass the many factories. I'd walk under this damp, dark, leering underpass on Linden Blvd. I never knew if my pace quickened from fear of someone who was lurking behind a wall or from the fear of seeing a rat scrambling for something to discover. My mother never knew I walked nearly three miles home every single day. I never told her...I never told Sonny that the school didn't give me a full fare pass, even though it was not feasible that I did not qualify for a free transportation card. I had to have qualified. I couldn't have been any poorer. I couldn't afford to pay the full fare. I couldn't even afford to pay half fare. Nevertheless, I can't explain why I never said anything. I guess I just didn't want to add to my mother's worries....her stress. So I sucked it up....but it sucked.

I never want to live such a life again.

I hated it. And I chose to fear it. And though it had the strength to bring me down, I didn't let it happen because somehow I knew that...

"Flowers grow out of darker moments." -Corita Kent

To say the least, I think I had a rough start. My first real memory in this world found me underneath the pillows of my mother's couch.

I was probably four years old at the time. I was sleeping on my mother's couch at about two o'clock in the morning, when there was this loud bang at the door. It startled me. The man who I thought was my father for many years later answered the door, only to be thrown away from the door by the two men who forced themselves in and all the way back to my mother's bedroom. I faintly remember getting up to peek at what was happening. I could hardly make out anything, but the vision that burns in my mind is the image of the phone wire being ripped from the wall.

I could hear my mother crying.

The image in my mind is foggy. I don't even remember creeping back to the couch, but I clearly remember hiding underneath the pillows. I must have shut my eyes so tightly that I fell asleep because the next thing I remember was standing quietly in the kitchen the next morning....my two aunts were speaking to the two police officers.....my mother sat on the kitchen chair, silent, as I stared at the drops of dried blood on the floor.

My mother's boyfriend was murdered that night and the two men who did it were never caught. So my mother and I had to move. And no one in my family, not until over thirty years later when I brought it up in a conversation with my Aunt Niameh, ever talked to me about what happened that night. I guess they thought I was too young to even be aware of what had happened that night, when in fact I was old enough. And much later in life, I would understand the impact of what had happened that night.

I spoke about that night in March 2013 in front of a captive audience. And I told them that I want to turn that "impact" into "inspiration", because I'm happy with how far I've come from what could have been a very tragic downward spiral so early in my life. When I think about it, being in the presence of a murder at the age of four years old could have led me to a life of crime, psychological damage that could have left me in a state of depression, anger, and aggression. But that didn't happen...for two main reasons: first, my family; my mother, my aunts Grace, Niameh, and Dottie; my cousins Theresa and Tyesha; their support, love, and guidance were my strength. And second, though I may not have been aware of it at the time...my very own mind.

I'm thankful for the way that I am wired. And I said before, scientific research shows that all of us can be re-wired in such a way that can help us rise from any situation, from any hardship, trauma, struggle, or obstacle.

I told one audience that I thank my mother and my family for not allowing a negative moment to get in the way of a positive future, a future where I can write a book about how I've put a positive spin on the events in my life to motivate myself and others to move forward.

We all have bumps along our metaphorical road that we fall over, and ditches in our metaphorical road that we fall into, and walls along our metaphorical road that we crash into. But no matter how many times we fall, no matter how deep we fall, and no matter how hard we get hit, I believe that we all have dreams of one day walking along that higher road of achievement. But the question is, 'How do we get pass this road to get to where we want to go?' Well, the first answer is we have to find a plan because there is no achievement without action. And the second thing we need to do is develop a positive mentality because with a positive mind, we can reach the elevation of our success.

By the way, for years afterwards, for nearly half of my life, I never knew whether that man who was murdered that night was my father. It wasn't until the last night I spent in our second Brooklyn apartment, before I moved to a small place in the West Village and my mother moved in with Aunt Grace, that I discovered a letter written by the man who I thought was my father. The letter was hidden underneath a pile of papers in a drawer. My mother had kept it for over twenty years. It had a few pieces of identification and several stamps from Ghana. The letter was originally mailed from Monrovia, Liberia.

July 11, 1976

My dearest Joe Joe,

I hope you and Markie are fine, and missing me as I miss you. Kisses. Well I am out here making a living and missing you very much. I think about us often and miss loving you and playing with our son.

This is our third port we have been to so far, and we have four more to go then home.

I hope you have told no one about me leaving, and I hope you are doing what I told you about keeping certain people who mean us no good out of our business.

Please put my suitcase in your closet for no one to see.

22

Do not tell our business to no one.

I love you Joe Joe, so please try and bear with me. I am yours and I belong to no other woman. I will write soon again.

As soon as you read this, answer right away. My address is on the back of this page. Loving you.

P.S. Answer right away so that I can read one letter before I start home. Send it airmail.

I love you Baby and give my love to Markie.

       I never spoke to my mother about that letter. The first person I ever shared that letter with was my wife, almost seventeen years after my mother passed away. I'm sure a psychologist would question why I've kept the letter and still profess that I am not curious, nor interested in investigating further. After all, he could have been my father. But he probably wasn't. Another document I found in my mother's drawer stated that my father was John Doe and his address was unknown. So yes, there is some level of curiosity, but nothing deep enough to interest me to explore. And I only choose to share it, because it is a part of my story…it's a part of the reflection of my past that makes me appreciate how far I've come.

I could have been another statistic.

The following are statistics from a website called The Fatherless Generation.

- 63% of youth suicides are from fatherless homes (US Dept. Of Health/Census) – 5 times the average.
- 90% of all homeless and runaway children are from fatherless homes – 32 times the average.
- 85% of all children who show behavior disorders come from fatherless homes – 20 times the average. (Center for Disease Control)

BEYOND LIMITATIONS

- 80% of rapists with anger problems come from fatherless homes –
  14 times the average. (Justice & Behavior, Vol. 14, p. 403-26)
- 71% of all high school dropouts come from fatherless homes –
  9 times the average. (National Principals Association Report)

I survived the statistics. I beat the odds. I've heard this said many different ways: life is not a product of destiny, but rather a product of design.

With that said, yes, I am puzzled by a letter that asked my illiterate mother to read it and write back. I'd be lying if I said I wasn't a little curious. I have some questions. My life has some unanswered questions, but I chose to believe that my mother and my family had their reasons for keeping me in the dark. I trust their decision. And I choose to accept that as the years passed, it was a memory that my family preferred not to revisit.

It took nearly thirty years, but I finally asked. My Aunt Niameh was very open about the incident. But there wasn't much she could add to the story. But she did confirm that the man who had been murdered that night was not my father. That still remains a mystery.

As I stood in that kitchen, drops of blood on the floor, I stood by my mother's side and I never thought about whom that man was. All I understood was that we were moving. A new life began for me, in another area of Brooklyn: East New York, Brooklyn, the area that had the highest murder rate in New York City. I don't think it was like that when we moved there, but it definitely became that by the time we left. It was a tough upbringing.

My mother was illiterate and on welfare. Before I was in the first grade, she let a new man move into our apartment. I knew he wasn't my father, but I let everyone believe otherwise. It was easier that way. One of my closest friends didn't know the truth until years after Sonny died. When Sonny was alive, he lost his roofing job, which was only on a need-to-hire-basis. And so, he lived off of our welfare. He wore the same clothes, sat in the same chair, and rolled cigarettes using the tobacco from used cigarette butts found in the staircase. He used to send me fishing in the staircase for those used cigarette butts. And then he would use torn pages from the Yellow Pages phone book to make his phony cigarettes. He drank too. And soon my mother drank with him…they drank a lot…they drank too much. I felt like I was watching my mother deteriorate. It was hard watching my mother hang out with the men in the parking lot behind our building, getting drunk. Sadly, I remember that glazed look in her eyes as she staggered through the door and down the hallway to her room. I think that's why I had a deep hatred for Sonny. I blamed him for doing this to my mother. I hated what he did to her. I hated that she allowed it. But I think I understand why it happened. My mother was afraid to be alone. Considering what brought us to the Pink Houses from Red Hook, I understood. Sonny was a strong and fearless man. She didn't have to be afraid anymore. I didn't have to be afraid anymore.

But I soon developed a fear of Sonny. He wasn't abusive, but he was intimidating. Soon, I became resentful and angry. So many things that he did or didn't do made me angry. It made me angry the day I walked into the house with my brand new Alvin and the Chipmunks album, an album that I bought with the money I made from picking up groceries for a few neighbors; he told me to return it to the store; he told me to give him the money so that he could buy a bottle of Thunderbird. It made me angry years later when he sent my mother into my room to ask me for money and I said no because I knew he had sent her and I knew why he had sent her. So he stormed into my room and demanded the money. And I gave it to him, because I was afraid.

But nothing my made me hate him more than the day when he knocked my mother to the ground after she backed our car into a parked car. Sonny had just bought a used car. It was blocking someone else's car. He wasn't home. My mother meant well. But she couldn't drive. SLAM! Sonny arrived on the scene shortly after. I don't think we had the car for two weeks. I don't think it took more than two minutes for a friend to tell me that Mr. Sonny had knocked my mother down to the ground. I hated him, sometimes.

And yet other times, I felt so protected around him. He wasn't my father, but he was a father figure. He was the one who weathered

25

through a blizzard to pick me up from school. He was the one who watched me from the window of our eighth floor apartment as I stood my ground against a bully who tried to force me to bend down and clean his sneakers. Sonny often watched over me from that eighth floor window. He had my back. He had our back. For what it's worth, he was a part of my family. And though my stories of Sonny cause people to villain-ize him, I'm actually glad he was around for nearly 10 years of my life.

We could spend a lot of energy hoarding hatred and holding grudges, but research shows that anger has a detrimental effect on our brains.

An article titled "Effects of Anger: What Anger Does to Your Body and Brain" on the website ScienceDaily covered a study conducted by scientists at the University College London. It stated, "The effects of anger and stress on the brain cannot be ignored. There is evidence that chronic stress can alter brain function at the cellular level…Stress and anger jeopardize the brain's ability to slow down…New studies also suggest that stress can cause neurons to shrink and disconnect. In short, stress promotes the death of neurons, which can explain why stress is the leading cause of depression.

Yes, it is healthy to release anger. Repressing anger can be detrimental. But we can't afford to let that anger consume us, regardless of the situation. As I always like to say, "Don't be a slave to your emotions. Be a master of your mind." We need to protect the mind, and in turn protect the body, so that we can protect what it is we really hope to achieve in life. Admittedly, that was difficult because life would not stop throwing at me more than I believe a young child should have to deal with.

I was only fifteen years old when Sonny died. It was already the fourth time in my life that I had experience dealing with death. After what I had witnessed at four years old, I had to deal with the pain of mourning my aunt Dottie. Later, I would mourn the untimely death of a high school friend. And that was the same year Sonny passed. When Sonny died, I became scared again. I had to become the man of the house. I had to protect my mother.

BEYOND LIMITATIONS

I'll never forget the day Sonny died. The night before, he was up late, complaining about a pain in his stomach. I heard him groan. I walked into the living room to find him lying on the floor, grimacing. He said he would be fine. So I went back to bed. In the morning, he was still on the floor, sleeping. I had to go to school late that day because I had a doctor's appointment. I was going to go to school after the appointment, but I had to go back home first. Sonny was still on the floor. My mother was sitting in the kitchen...again. Somehow, she knew. I went to her room to get a pair of glasses. I put the lenses up against Sonny's nose and mouth. I was hoping to see a film of air pressed against the lens. I never saw it. He wasn't breathing. I called my aunt Grace. She told me to call 911. I called 911 and said that my father was having a heart attack. I called Sonny's sister and told her the news.

I don't remember saying much to my mother. I don't remember her saying much to me, or anyone else. I spoke to the paramedics. My mother wasn't a woman of many words, hardly any. She didn't have to say a word that day. She knew.

This is the first time I've really thought about this from my mother's point of view. She lost so much. She was alone again....scared again....taking care of an only son.....a fatherless son....a son on welfare...a son in a neighborhood that was getting more dangerous by the day....a son with an illiterate mother. I feel for her now that I see her moments through her eyes. She must have been so scared. She had her sisters, but she must have felt alone.

And being poor couldn't have helped. I can only imagine how she felt on the many days she needed me to walk with her to her face-to-face meetings. We lived four train stops away. The bus ride was thirty minutes away from our house. But we walked. That's all we could afford to do. On a good day, we walked one way, and took the bus back. But usually, we walked both ways. Scrounging for enough change just to take the bus one way was not a humbling experience; it was an experience filled with shame, tears being held back. But there was no time to cry. We got whatever coins we could get so we could continue to get the food stamps we needed. And I remember walking to the Check Cashing Place afterwards, only to hear the woman behind the window, every single time, ask my mother to sign her name, only to hear my mother respond that she could only sign with an "x".

Life was so unfortunate.

And we were so vulnerable.

When I was in school, I worried when my mother went to the store. How did she know the difference between a five-dollar bill and a twenty-dollar bill or a one-dollar food stamp from a ten-dollar food stamp? Someone would take advantage of her, like our neighbor's daughter who took my mother to cash her welfare check, only to take most of the money. My mother knew she was a victim, but what could we do?

By this point, my neighborhood was the worst. I peeked out the window one night to hear the sounds of a vicious argument. From my eighth floor window, I hid my face behind the wall of the windowpane so that no one could see me watching. They were teasing this one boy. He must have been drunk or high. He took out a gun and started shooting. I don't know if my mother was awake or not. We never talked about it. The boy lived in the apartment down the hall from us. We knew his mother well. She was the one who years prior got into a fight with another neighbor and used a phone to crack the other woman's head open. I was still young then, presumably too young to notice, but not too young to see Sonny taking the battered woman to our shower to wash away the blood. No one ever talked to me about that either.

My mother and I never talked much, but we were inseparable. I pride myself to this day on being a Momma's Boy. I want my sons to be momma's boys. I even want my little girl to be a momma's girl. One of my fondest memories of my mother was riding the bus, going home from my aunt Grace's house. I was so tired that my head slumped on to my mother's shoulders. She was my rock, not solid enough, but sturdy enough…comforting enough. In the midst of the pain, the shame, and the struggle, I loved…I mean I love…my "mommy" more than can be imagined. And it is my love for her that made me dream.

BEYOND LIMITATIONS

But I remember when my mommy, often described as my roommate by a very close friend, barked at me like a typical parent, which wasn't so typical for her, because the pain had finally consumed her. She came home drunk, the first time since Sonny had died. I barked at her for drinking. That's when she said the words I'll never forget, "I'm the parent; you're the child." So I went to my room. I could not bring myself to respond. I think I understood the pain behind that anger. It had been a year since Sonny had died.

And when my uncle in South Carolina invited my mother to move in with him, she accepted the offer. I couldn't believe it, especially since it was my senior year of high school. But even though it was meant to be a permanent move, it was only a short visit. After her return, she started to become dependant on different medicines. Years later while I was still in college, after her stay at the hospital, my mother moved in with my aunt. I, on the other hand, moved into my own apartment.

Finally, we had emerged from life in the projects. We had survived.

With that came the accomplishment of graduating from college and graduate school. My greatest memory was one that I did not see. My aunt Grace sat with my mother in the balcony of Carnegie Hall. She told me how my mother cried as she watched me walk across that stage. The son of an illiterate mother- now a college graduate from a prestigious, private school in New York City, New York University, with a bachelor's degree in English Literature and a Masters in Speech Communication, the credentials to become a high school teacher.

After I got my teaching job at my old high school in February 1996, my mother became ill while visiting my aunt Niameh. She was admitted to and never left NYU Hospital. The last time I saw my mommy was when I watched her from the doorway of her hospital room, before a road trip to Atlanta. Before I left the hospital that night, the nurse brought in a meal. I remember holding my mother's hand as I watched *The Young & The Restless* on the mounted television. That's how my mother and I often bonded when I was home from school, watching her favorite soap opera. That day I felt like I was watching it by myself. My mother had a glazed look in her eye. So I unwrapped her food and I spoon-fed my mother. And that is when the thought occurred to me that life had come full circle. She brought me into this world, feeding a speechless child. And there I was feeding my speechless mother; little did I know that she was leaving this world.

I live with a lot of pain. And I live with this regret: that I never got to purchase that large home for my mommy and her two sisters, that my mommy didn't live to hold her three grandchildren in her arms. But she did live to see me become a teacher. And as she looks down on me now, she smiles because I am now the Assistant Principal of English at one of the top schools in the nation. How proud must my mommy be!

And how tearful was it when my wife and I brought my oldest son to the cemetery when he was just under 3 years old, and he said to his grandmother, "I'll see you later."

I smiled.

And I'm sure my mother smiled too.

My mother has a lot to smile about, and I do too….because we emerged…we made it through…

But I'm not done yet. I'm still not where I want to be. There are still aspects of my past life that I'm afraid to see continue. There are visions of what I endured in my childhood that I'm afraid to have my children experience. So I choose to use that fear to my advantage.

Fear is a powerful motivator, not only for instinctual survival, but also for those who fear so badly what they don't want to experience in their lives, that they become motivated to work hard towards changing their lives. Whenever I'm asked to mentor a young person who lacks the motivation and drive to do his work, I talk to him about the consequences of not making an effort. We must compare the consequences of living the life we should fear with the benefits of the life we desire and do exactly what fear makes us do in survival mode: back us into a corner and force us to attack.

"He who is not everyday conquering some fear has not learned the secret of life." - Ralph Waldo Emerson

BEYOND LIMITATIONS

"Fear is nature's warning signal to get busy." - *Henry C. Link*

So let's use fear of the undesirable to chase what we desire.

Using fear of the undesirable to chase what you desire: I call that embracing the struggle: I call that taking negativity and infusing a positive charge. Many, if not all of us, have lived through experiences that we just want to leave behind. But so many people never move forward because they convince themselves that there is no escape; they believe that their past has created an inescapable pattern. They've accepted their "so-called fate". They label those who have made it through as "lucky." But I don't call that luck. I call it drive, a drive motivated by an unwillingness and by a fear to continue to live with the cards that we have been dealt.

The following are just a few examples from an article I read called "Wrong Side of the Tracks: 10 Celebrities who Overcame their Pasts". *(http://www.customizedgirl.com/blog/?p=397)*

I once read that Jim Carrey lived a difficult life in Canada with his three siblings and out of work parents. Carrey's father accepted a job offer at a tire factory that wanted to hire the entire family. In exchange, Carrey's family was allowed to live in a small building next to the factory. But eventually, his family, feeling defeated, left the factory and ended up homeless. They moved into a van and Jim began performing at a comedy club called Yuk Yuks. In the early 1980s, Carrey moved to L.A. and began performing at the legendary club The Comedy Store. One night comedian Keenan Ivory Wayans came to see a show and ended up casting Carrey in the now classic comedy show "In Living Color." Jim Carrey rose beyond the fear and the struggle.

I also read that Oprah Winfrey was born in rural, poverty-stricken Mississippi to two teenage parents. She grew up mostly with her dirt-poor grandmother on a farm. When she got a little older, Oprah decided to move up to Wisconsin to be with her mother. But once she got there, she was repeatedly molested by male relatives. Traumatized, Oprah turned to drugs, alcohol and sex and gave birth to a premature baby when she was

31

just 14. The baby died soon after birth. She then decided to move in with her father in Nashville, where she got her start as a reporter with a local TV station. In just a few years, she was promoted to co-anchor and, soon after, the host of a local talk show. In 1984, she landed a national talk show spot in Chicago, competing in the ratings with Phil Donahue. Oprah Winfrey rose beyond the fear and the struggle.

And then there's the story of Curtis Jackson. Born to a cocaine-dealing, 15-year-old mother, 50 Cent, had it bad. His mother dealt cocaine until she was murdered when 50 Cent was 8. She died after someone drugged her drink and then gassed her apartment with her in it. Fatherless, Jackson then moved in with his grandmother and his eight aunts and uncles. He said this was the moment he turned to the streets. At 11, he started selling crack. By the age of 12, he was carrying drugs and a gun with him to school. He began getting arrested in the mid 1990s for drugs and served six months in prison. In 2000, Jackson was rapping locally in New York and getting attention, but he still didn't have a record deal. One day, he was sitting in a friend's car outside his grandmother's house when another car pulled up and a gunman shot Jackson nine times at close range, putting him in the hospital. After his recovery, Jackson put out an independently produced tape, which caught the attention of Eminem. Eminem signed Jackson as 50 Cent and in 2003 Jackson became a star. Since then he's put out 4 multi-platinum albums. Curtis Jackson rose beyond the fear and the struggle.

Now I don't necessarily define success, or reaching the other side of the obstacle, by "the riches" one may earn, but I do find inspiration in these "rags to riches" stories. It's proof that regardless of the struggle, if you don't let it get the best of you, you can find the strength within the struggle, the strength to pursue and achieve.

So here's what I want you to do right now. Go get a pen, a pencil, or a notepad app on your phone or tablet. And then use your words to create the visual of what it is you fear will happen if you don't push yourself to make a difference in your life….if you don't push yourself to make a change in your life. Share in writing the past you fear returning to….put in writing the consequences of continuing to live the status quo. I don't intend to imply that we cannot be happy with what we have currently, but if we want more out of life, then we must look directly into the face of the life that we don't want to live for the rest of our lives and then remind ourselves that we have shown the strength to endure what has been handed us. And now we can turn the power to endure into the power to progress.

"Don't' let the low times keep you down. Learn from them and reach for the high times." - David Wiemers

"Square your shoulders to the world, be not the kind to quit; It's not the load that weighs you down but the way you carry it that lifts you up." – Anonymous.

Chapter Three: Do It For Them

"You will find, as you look back on your life, that the moments that stand out are the moments when you have done things for others."
-Henry Drummond

Yes, you should aspire to do it for yourself;
But the impact of your glory will shine brighter
When those around you are lifted
By the warmth of your sunrays;
Who is that person in your life?
Be motivated by the desire to see those,
Who are closest to you,
Prosper.

The greatest dream I ever imagined will forever be my greatest dream unfulfilled. I can't give you the exact picture because I'm no interior designer, but the image is of a big white house, something like a mansion, the place I wanted to get for my mother, my aunt Grace, and my aunt Niameh, a place where the three sisters could live, comfortably, happily, with no concerns, no worries, no responsibilities, for the rest of their lives.

When I reflect on that dream, I'm reminded of the night when I watched an episode of 106 & Park, when hosts Rocsi and Terrence J asked rapper Ace Hood what he did with his first paycheck. He answered that he gave his mother a Louis Vutton purse. And when she looked inside, she was surprised to see $10,000. He bought her a house and she never had to work a day in her life ever since. And then I'm reminded of that Oprah special when after interviewing Rihanna, she invited Rihanna's mother to a glorious dream home, a home Rihanna's mother was seeing for the first time, a home that her superstar, pop star daughter purchased for her. It was beautiful. It was beautiful what Rihanna was able to do for her mother.

BEYOND LIMITATIONS

For most of my life, my star was right by my side: my mommy. And now, my star is beyond the sky. And yet, she still continues to be a reason why I do what I do. We need those reminders…the reasons why we do what we do…why we strive to achieve.

One day, I was a little fed up at work (to those who know me: believe it or not, yes, that happens to me too; it just doesn't consume me. I won't allow that. And neither should anyone else). Anyway, as I was feeling a little fed up, I reminded myself why I do what I do. I looked at the school website to see the images of the kids. That's whom I work for; that's who reminds me to keep going!

I guess that's why when I talk to any of them, especially those who struggle, I implore them to think about how what they're doing, or in some cases, not doing, makes their mothers feel. I'm such a momma's boy, and such a proud one, that I pull the mother card a lot. But I shouldn't assume that for everyone, it's your mother. It might be someone else. It might be many others. What I should do is ask them to identify for themselves, who that person is for whom they want to do well.

Who is that person in your life?

I wish I had kept my college essay and framed it, because it truly expresses my belief that as important as it is to have role models, it's equally, if not more important to have someone who is your inspiration, a person for whom you would do anything, to whom you would want to give anything.

I recently found a birthday card that I had given to my mother. I wrote:

Dear Mommy,

Everything I've done

Everything I do

And everything I will do

Will be inspired by you

BEYOND LIMITATIONS

You are my inspiration

My motivation

You are the air I breathe

And every dream I fulfill

Will be because of you.

I love you!

Nearly ten years after my mother passed, my new family was born, beginning with my marriage and then the subsequent birth of my three children. What that means to me is that the greatest dream I ever conceived has found a new focus and will become the greatest dream fulfilled for a new source of inspiration in my life.

I never understood why people kept pictures of their families on their desks, but now I do it proudly. But I don't do it to show off my family (though they are beautiful) and I don't do it because that's just what people do (that's always a bad reason). I do it because I firmly believe that a driving force in the pursuit of our dreams is the reminder of why we aspire. Of course, you, yourself, should always be the first reason, but that other person or people in your life can do wonders for your motivation. My mother, my aunt Grace, and my aunt Niameh motivated me. They inspired me.

My mother (Johanna) watered the seed; she taught me one of the most motivational lessons that I share to this day: if you're not willing to do it yourself, then you don't really want it. I'll elaborate later.

My aunt (Grace) provided the sunlight: everyone loved her and she loved everyone. I watched her feed an entire extended family on holidays. I watched her smile and wave to everyone on the street. I credit her for inspiring my phrase, "Have a Safe, Pleasant, and Positive Day."

BEYOND LIMITATIONS

My aunt (Niameh) is the toughest woman I know. She's the ground on which the flower stands. She has such a no-non-sense personality. She is unwavering in her convictions. She's such a sweet person, but she's a brick wall if you dare charge or challenge her. I think of her when I think of being a rock for my own family.

These three precious women will always be my sources of inspiration.

And now there's my wife Lauren and my three kids, Jordan, Sydney, and Dylan. I often stay up until 2am working on speeches, drafting my book, building my professional speaking business, and attending to my school administrative duties. People often ask me where all this energy comes from. Some of it is natural. And some of it is driven by my dream for my family.

One summer, I sat on the steps of my cousins' house in Queens, New York; I sat next to Jordan who told me that one day he wants to live in a house with stairs outside, stairs inside, an attic, and a backyard. That wasn't the first time he ever shared that dream with me. And I think about his dream every time I get one of those emails from Averne By the Sea. I save those emails so that I have a vision of what I want to provide for my oldest little man. I'm still waiting for Sydney and Dylan to communicate their dreams so that I can add them to my list of inspirations.

According to Dan Batson, author of The Altruism Question: Toward a Social Psychological Answer, the empathy-altruism hypothesis claims that empathic concern (other-oriented emotion felt for someone in need—sympathy, compassion, tenderness, and the like) produces altruistic motivation (a motivational state with the ultimate goal of increasing the other's welfare)."

BEYOND LIMITATIONS

So here's the next thing I want you to do. Identify who that person is, the person who's welfare you'd like to improve with the power of your achievements, and take a picture of him or her or them, make it your screen saver or buy a frame, and put the picture where you look most often. The greatest power of any achievement is the infectious joy it can bring. Always keep in your mind and in your sight those, including yourself of course, who will benefit from your success. And let them be your motivation.

"As my mother says, "You give back, you don't give up." You can always choose to help others. If you do, it will change you."
-Susan Ford

Chapter Four: Confirm Your Commitment

"The difference between a successful person and others is not lack of strength nor a lack of knowledge but rather a lack of will."
–Vince Lombardi

If you are not willing to do something to get what you want,
Then you don't really want it.
We must be motivated by a true desire and willingness
To get what we say we want.

-words inspired by Johanna Williams

I once read a short work that expresses that everything we truly need to know in life, we learned in kindergarten. How true that is, is surely subjective, but the point is not about classes in macroeconomics, biochemistry, or software technology. The message is about life's most important lessons. And how important are life lessons? That's rhetorical indeed. They're so invaluable that I treasure what my mother taught me about life more than anything she could not teach me. I learned my multiplication table from a kid who lived down the hall from us. He gave me a blank table at about 6pm and told me that he wanted to see the answers the next morning. I think I was only in the first grade at the time. I stayed up until I think midnight, going from 1x1 to 10x10. What an accomplishment. I thank Felix for that challenge and achievement. I learned about certain animals whenever Sonny would quiz me about something he saw on PBS. And even when I didn't know the answer, he implored me to sit down and watch the program with him so I could learn. I thank him for pushing me to learn. Mrs. McIntyre taught me long division. Dr. Weinberger taught me how to delve deeper into literature. Mr. Trout and Professor Greene taught me how to speak in public. All those academic lessons were great. My mother could not have taught me any of them. But those lessons paled in comparison to the valuable lesson she did teach me, so valuable that I repeat it to my children all the time and I share it with my students every opportunity I get.

BEYOND LIMITATIONS

"If you don't want to work for what you want, then you don't really want it."

That taught me to either work hard towards whatever I said I wanted, or to change course if I wasn't really motivated to do whatever it took to get whatever I thought I wanted, because maybe, I didn't want it as badly as I thought I did. I either had to reevaluate or self-motivate.

It all began with a simple question:

"Mommy, can you make a bowl of cereal?"

Her response was simple: "Make it yourself."

"But I don't want to make it."

Her final words, "Then you don't really want it."

And there you have it. My mother couldn't give me scholarship, but she gave me the single most important lesson in my life. Had it not been for that lesson she taught me when I was about 12 years old, if not younger, then I never would have become a teacher.

When I was in college, I wanted to study journalism. I wanted to be a broadcast journalist. So I enrolled in the Introduction to Journalism course at NYU. I admit that I didn't take the course seriously, as I should have. After all, wasn't this what I wanted to do? Well towards the end of the term, we had to take an exam on what we studied from the textbook (the same textbook I half-heartedly read). Before the professor gave us our scores, he announced in a large lecture hall that someone in the class scored a 39 on the exam. At that point, I turned to my friend Dan and joked about the fool who scored so low (what a moron!) Well I don't have to tell you whom the moron turned out to be. When I got my final grade in the class, it was a D. My counselor informed me that if I wanted to major in journalism, I would have to retake the class.

"But I don't want to retake the class," I thought to myself.

BEYOND LIMITATIONS

And then my mother's words revisited my mind. I guess if I didn't want to retake the class, then I didn't really want to be a broadcast journalist. And so I changed my major and pursued a degree in English with a focus on Writing. Then I heard about an opportunity to double major in Education. With that, I refocused my English studies on Literature, and the rest is history.

And the fact that my mother passed away the summer after I got my opportunity to teach at the school where I would eventually become the Assistant Principal of English makes her words even more meaningful to me. I'd like to think that her words guided me, which is all a parent could ever hope for.

Now sometimes I do wonder: maybe I just wasn't mature enough to push myself to retake that class and pursue a career as a broadcast journalist; but I have no regrets. I only have an appreciation for the most important life-changing lesson I learned from my mother. Maybe Robert Fulghum learned his lessons in kindergarten, but I learned mine in my mother's kitchen.

In life, we will have a lot of dreams and we may chase many of them. But there comes a time along the chase when we will have to answer that essential question: Do we really want it? That is when our convictions are tested the most. Either we must dig deep and find the motivation we need to achieve or we must reevaluate our desire to fulfill that dream. By the way, reevaluating is not the equivalent of quitting. Sometimes, we waste a lot of time being stubborn about finishing something that we have no desire to do. Success isn't necessarily achieved by staying on the road. Often, it's achieved by knowing when to redirect your travel plans. And sometimes, we confuse our desire to have something with our desire to get something. By the way, getting somebody else to do what we say we want to do doesn't cut it. Some may want to call that management, but in this case, it's laziness. But you're not lazy. Lazy people just say they want it, but never get up to get it because they're too....well...lazy. And laziness simply translates to a lack of desire and will. And remember, the key to success is the desire and the willingness. Without willingness, there is no true desire. And without desire and willingness, there is no meaningful action. And in turn, there is no success.

As Rev Run once tweeted, "Do what you gotta to do so you can do what you wanna do."

In closing, though my mother's words convinced me that when our willingness to do what it takes to get what we want doesn't exist, we have to question our desires, her words were moreso a push to get me to do what it takes to get what I say I want. After all, I did make that bowl of cereal. I really did want it. My mommy just taught me to go and get it...to get it myself.

I read an article (*5 Ways Willingness Helps You Achieve Your Dreams*), on PaigeandBrian.com, that stated, *"Willingness is the first step in birthing our dreams. It is that amazing state of mind that allows our dreams to grow into fruition."*

It's time to take out that pad and pencil or that notebook app again. First, answer the question: What is it that you specifically want to do? And be very specific. If you want to be independently wealthy, that's great, but what is it that you must do in order to make that happen. By the way, the research says that if you want to be independently wealthy, you have to first cut your expenses by 30%-50%. That may sound like a lot, and I don't think I'm there yet, but when I started walking to work and walking home every day, I started saving $100 per month in commuter expenses. And once I started making my lunch, I cut down on the frivolous spending on fast food and junk food. I have yet to sit down and calculate what percent of my expenses I have cut, but now I'm motivated to do so. Sure it would be nice if I had someone who could just give me the money that I would like to have to fulfill my dreams for my family, so that I wouldn't have to make sacrifices. But most of us don't have that luxury. So we must do it ourselves. And even if we did have that luxury, it would come at a price; it would cost the greatest sacrifice: our motivation to achieve on our own. And that cannot be something we should ever sacrifice. Writing this book has been one of the most enduring tasks I've ever tried. Sometimes I questioned whether or not the sleepless hours, the constant reading and rewriting was worth it, but it has been. And it has been, simply because it was something I really wanted to do. (And I imagine often that my mother is smiling in heaven as she turns to read each page. Thank you mommy for inspiring me. Thank you for teaching me that whatever the goal is that I say I want to achieve, I must figure out how to get it done and then do it.)

I once told a group of peers that it's not good enough just to have a destination, because if you really want to go somewhere, then you have to have navigation. In other words, you need a well-defined, well-plotted, and well-calculated plan to get to where you want to go. But even the navigation isn't enough. You also need activation. So then ask yourself if you are willing to do what you say you want to do to get to where you want to be. No one is looking over your shoulder, so you can be honest with yourself. It's easy to say we are willing to do something. But we don't have to say it, if we know it's not true. If it's not true, then think again about something else you actually are willing to do. Once again, write down exactly what it is you want to do and outline the steps you must take to do it. And then place that list in a place where you can see it daily so you can constantly drive yourself to get it. And remember, accomplish one step at a time and celebrate each victory along the way. I know we all say that is cliché advice, but it's only become cliché advice because many people have had the will to do it and then stopped doing it, saying it doesn't work when the truth is they never kept up the habit of doing it. Think about it, what does it mean to have will power? It doesn't just mean that you have the desire. It also means that you have the plan and the persistence to complete the practice.

On New Year's Day 2013, I posted this message, "There are so many jokes about failed attempts to keep New Year's Resolutions. Regardless, every new year, is a new attempt...a fresh start...another opportunity...a renewed energy. So I want to wish all of us a Positive, Productive, Safe, and Successful 2013. The new year is a recharge for our mental batteries. So let's Ride the Momentum. Let's choose one well defined goal and one regular habit towards achieving that goal. And let's start doing it today."

BEYOND LIMITATIONS

Right now, I want you to take a break from reading just so you can do the next four steps. Just remember where you put the book, so you can continue reading later. This book is a resource, but you are the force.

1. Write down your goal. *(I want to write a book.)*

2. Research and determine the necessary steps to make it happen. *(Step One: Summarize your purpose and then outline your message into potential chapters.)*

3. Ask yourself honestly if you are willing to do what it takes to achieve that goal. *(YES!!!!)*

4. And if the answer is yes, then start the first task. *(Sit down for 30 minutes today and freewrite.)*

"Where the willingness is great the difficulties cannot be great"
-Niccole Machiavelli

"It doesn't matter how much you want. What really matters is how much you want it. The extent and complexity of the problem does not matter as much as does the willingness to solve it." -Ralph Marston

"I hope I have convinced you / the only thing that separates successful people from the ones who aren't is the willingness to work very, very hard." - Helen Gurley Brown

Chapter Five: Keep Yourself Busy

"In times of great stress or adversity, it's always best to keep busy, to plow your anger and your energy into something positive." -Lee Iacocca

Keep yourself busy to stay out of trouble.
We must be motivated by the consequences of inaction.
-words inspired by Teresa Arthur

If I could've kept that bag of noodles for the rest of my life, I would have found a way to save the package and memorialize it. When I was about 14 years old, I went on a three-day hiking trip through the Appalachian trails. It was me, maybe 9 other kids, and two summer camp counselors. I actually signed up to do this. And though I don't remember many details (after all, all we did was hike, sleep, and eat...a lot of pasta apparently), that experience will be one of the most memorable, and meaningful moments in my life. I never would have imagined doing that only a few summers prior. It all was because my beloved cousins Teresa and Tyesha, two of the many additional mothers I've been fortunate to have in my life, decided that they were going to send me and my cousins Damian, Michael, and Robert to sleep-away camp. The first summer was two weeks. The next was four weeks. The third was six weeks. And that last summer was for the entire summer, eight whole weeks. And at some point or another, during those many summers, I went on a three-day hike, competed in a week-long camp-style Olympics, played tennis, roasted marshmallows, rowed a boat, and went fishing. I did things I never would have done had I stayed home for the summer. Teresa and Tyesha knew it was best to keep us busy and exposed to something different. And my mother simply agreed to let me go. And that was the best thing she ever agreed to because, as Teresa always taught (and this is exactly why she wanted to send us to camp), it's best to keep busy so you can stay out of trouble. That was the mantra that became the backbone of what I now consider one of my essential qualities: my productive work ethic.

BEYOND LIMITATIONS

I firmly believe that we must be motivated by the consequences of inaction. That's why we must keep busy. That is why we must be productive. Had it not been for my summer camp experience, I may have become another statistic.

I read an article by the Afterschool All-stars that read, *"[Young people] who do not participate in after school programs are nearly three times more likely to skip classes or use marijuana or other drugs; they are also more likely to drink alcohol, smoke cigarettes and engage in sexual activity...Young people with nothing to do during out-of-school hours miss valuable chances for growth and development. The odds are high that youth with nothing positive to do and nowhere to go will find things to do that negatively influence their development and futures."*

I'm glad I went to sleep-away camp. I'm glad that I ran track in elementary school. I'm glad that I performed in my high school musicals. I'm glad I had a job while I was in college. And I'm glad that I'm a member of Toastmasters International. Yes, even as an adult, I'm doing extra activities.

I can't say with certainty that I would have definitely become the productive, hardworking person that I am today if it had not been instilled in me that keeping busy is a pathway not only from trouble, but also and most importantly towards being successful.

In closing, breaks are necessary. Relaxation is necessary. But free time is instrumental to productivity for only so long before it becomes counterproductive. So take whatever project you're working on and set aside a regular amount of time to work on it. And also, identify other things you can do with your time: hobbies or recreational organizations. I have had the greatest time participating in my Toastmasters meetings. I've met and networked with great people. I've been motivated and inspired by other people. I have learned things from other people and also had the privilege to teach and share ideas with other people. And the best part is I love delivering presentations. So yes, I give up two nights a month when I could be sitting on the couch watching a game or a favorite show, but that wouldn't contribute to my plans and my aspirations.

Besides, according to an article written by Sarah Klein for CNN, *"The more time you spend watching TV, the greater your risk of dying at an earlier age -- especially from heart disease, researchers found. Each additional hour spent in front of the TV increased the risk of dying from heart disease by 18 percent and the overall risk of death by 11 percent, according to the study, [by the American Heart Association]. 'Prolonged watching of television equals a lot of sitting, which invariably means there's an absence of muscle movement,' David Dunstan, Ph.D. says. 'If your muscles stay inactive for too long, it can disrupt your metabolism,' he explains. 'Studies show that television leads to an increase in the consumption of energy-dense, snack-type foods,' he says. 'It's a stimulus for poor dietary behavior, whereas some of the other types of sedentary behavior are less likely to stimulate poor snacking behaviors. And because it burns so few calories -- about the same as sleeping, hour for hour -- watching TV tends to reduce a person's overall energy output,' Dunstan adds."* And the research shows the same effects occur when we sit in front of a computer for hours at a time, whether that's at home or at work.

Furthermore, *according to J.L. Veerman and G.N. Healy,* "*research shows that people between the ages of 18 and 34 watch more than two hours of Internet or mobile video per week, in addition to the average 23 hours they spend tuned into live TV. And all this time watching TV, whether it's on the traditional tube or on a smartphone, may be taking a negative toll on our health. One study found that for every hour spent watching TV, our life expectancy decreases by 22 minutes.*"

Yes, we all need some moments of escape, some moments to vegetate, but don't let that rest consume you. If you do, then before you know it, your health will deteriorate and your time will be lost. And as my good friend Lou always says, the worst thing in life is wasted time, because unlike money, once the time is gone, you can never get it back. Don't lose your time. Don't lose yourself. Don't lose the chance to do something extraordinary. Create a habit of keeping yourself busy.

BEYOND LIMITATIONS

So here's what I want you to do right now: take a break from what I'm sharing with you and use the time to do a little research. Find an organization or activity that appeals to your interests and gets you out of the house, something that will help you develop a skill and a mentality that will empower your efforts to achieve your goals. Search. Join. Participate.

Stay busy. Stay productive.

And you will create a habit that will be key to your success.

"A man always has to be busy with his thoughts if anything is to be accomplished." -Antonie van Leeuwenhoek

"Determine never to be idle... It is wonderful how much may be done if we are always doing." -Thomas Jefferson

Chapter Six: Go Beyond Expectations

"The rung of a ladder was never meant to rest upon, but only to hold a man's foot long enough to enable him to put the other somewhat higher." -Thomas Henry Huxley

"We are kept from our goal not by obstacles but by a clear path to a lesser goal." -Robert Brault

Doing what you're not supposed to do is stupid,
But doing what you're supposed to do is not enough.
We must be motivated by what lies beyond the extra mile.

We must be motivated by the benefits of going the extra mile. Needless to say though, we are surrounded by examples of people doing things they're not supposed to do.

"A survey published at Getschooled.com cites data that as many as 7 million students - about 15% of the K-12 population - are out of school 18 or more days of the school year. And many of them don't think skipping school will impact their future. That's not in line with reality. The study points out that students who skip more than 10 days of school are significantly (about 20%) less likely to get a high school diploma. And they're 25% less likely to enroll in higher education." - Carl Azuz, CNN

The Partnership at Drugfree.org released a survey that found nearly 1 in 10 teens said they smoke marijuana at least 20 or more times a month. "Researchers found that adolescents who used marijuana at least four days per week lost an average of eight IQ points between the ages of 13 and 38. Heavy pot smokers tended to show deficits in memory, concentration, and overall brainpower in relation to their peers, but these problems were more pronounced -- and seemingly more lasting -- among those who picked up the habit as teens, the study found. An eight-point decline in IQ isn't negligible. Previous research suggests a drop in intelligence of that magnitude could, for instance, affect a

BEYOND LIMITATIONS

person's long-term career prospects, job performance and income." - Amanda Gardner, Health Magazine

"According to surveys in U.S. News and World Report: 80% of 'high-achieving' high school students admit to cheating; 51% of high school students did not believe cheating was wrong; 75% of college students admitted cheating, and 90% of college students didn't believe cheaters would be caught; and almost 85% of college students said cheating was necessary to get ahead. Furthermore, Professor Donald McCabe, leading expert in academic integrity, found the following: 72% of students reported one or more instances of serious cheating on written work; 15% had submitted a paper obtained in large part from a term paper mill or website; 52% had copied a few sentences from a website without citing the source; and over 45% admitted to collaborating inappropriately with others on assignments."

"On any given day in the United States, 18 percent of men and 11 percent of women drink more alcohol than federal guidelines recommend, according to a study that also found that 8 percent of men and 3 percent of women are full-fledged 'heavy drinkers'. 'Binge drinking (more than four drinks on any one day for men and more than three on any one day for women and older adults) even one time can increase the risk of injury from falls, motor vehicle accidents and other accidents,' said Jennifer Mertens, a research medical scientist at Kaiser Permanente Division of Research in Oakland, California" - Reuters

"In a new survey conducted by Harris Interactive, fully 28% of respondents said they would act immorally — including lying or backstabbing — to keep their jobs. Given the state of the economy, perhaps it comes as no big shock that 13% of the survey respondents said they would outright lie or exaggerate to keep their jobs — even though such behavior is forbidden by many companies' ethics policies. About 2% said they would take credit for someone else's work or flirt with the boss to get ahead, and 4% would lie about having common interests with their boss to deepen their bond with a superior." -Alice Park, TIME

BEYOND LIMITATIONS

Unfortunately, these are just some of the many examples of things that people are just not supposed to do.

When I was 13, I was horrified to see a gang of boys and girls on a city bus target a kid for no reason, other than "because it was fun". He sat there innocently, minding his own business, reading a book. I saw them out of the corner of my eyes, eyes desperately trying to avert so that they would not notice me. I saw them rise out of there seats like reverse dominoes, in formation, with intent. They surrounded him. They stood above him and eclipsed him. And then they kicked him and beat him, and humiliated him. The bus driver screamed for them to stop, but it was to no avail. They didn't even take anything from him. And as they crashed through the back door of the bus, the boy slumped in his seat, tears quivering down his face; his book lay face down on the floor of the bus.

Why do these things happen?

As a father, I pray that I never have to see any of my children walk through the door bruised and battered from something that just shouldn't happen.

When I was 20, travelling home from an abruptly shortened work day due to the threat of a rapidly spreading cross country riot, I was horrified to see a gang of kids on a subway car march their way towards an innocent white woman. They hovered over her suspecting body. As she cowered in a fetal position, the kids latched on to the pole above her seat and pummeled her, barking remarks about Rodney King and the LAPD.

And then it pains me to share that not only have I read about things people shouldn't do, not only have I witnessed stupid things, but I've been the victim as well.

One night after a few hours of "Youth Patrol: Youth on the Move", I agreed to walk a friend to the deli. As we crossed the street, I had a feeling we were being followed, so I looked behind us. There were five boys. They were surely following us. So I told my friend, "I think we're being followed." He didn't seem worried. So we walked into the deli. And so did the five boys. We never bought anything. We just walked down a few aisles. Their footsteps shadowed us. So we walked out of the deli and my friend said that we should walk to the next deli to see if we were really being followed. I thought it was pretty obvious, but I followed his lead. The gates of the next deli were down. The streets were dark. The blocks were empty. So we walked passed that deli. And they passed the deli too; it was confirmed. And unfortunately, the further we walked, the darker it loomed. We turned the corner to walk down an even darker street. Only one light was noticeable from a room of a two-story home. I was scared.

As I turned to look behind us, one boy shouted, "Whatchu looking at?"

Footsteps thundered into a chase. The next thing I knew an arm had wrapped itself around my neck. It squeezed so tightly that it had nearly suffocated me. I blacked out from the choke. When I came to, my face pressed against the concrete pavement, all I could see were these five boys kicking and beating my friend into the concrete pavement. As I pulled my body from the floor, I was warned to run away. One of my greatest regrets was heeding that warning. And yet, had I not heeded that warning, I may not be here today to write this book. My friend did make it out of there okay after they robbed him for his brand new shoes, but he quit Youth Patrol after that.

That was one of the stories I did confess to my mother, to Sonny, to aunt Grace. To my aunt Grace's dismay though, I continued to work for Youth Patrol. I stayed on even past the night when my cousin received his back-pay check. He had two checks that night, two checks and an appetite. So we walked to a nearby deli where he asked to cash one of the two checks, not the $15 check, but the $50 check. The man behind the counter said that he only had singles. As he counted the fifty singles, I noticed three or four boys standing outside the store. They didn't say a word to us as we stepped out of the store, in my cousin's hand a brown paper bag with a bottle of soda and a pack of Twinkies. They didn't say a word, but after several steps, I looked behind us and saw that we were being followed. They must have been scared themselves because we made it past three or four blocks without a pounce. But then my cousin whispered to me, "On the count of three, run!" I was game; after all, I had been on the track team since the second grade. The only thing that slowed me down was the book bag I was carrying. I could have escaped, but I stopped in the middle lane of Linden Boulevard because I couldn't leave my cousin. As this kid grabbed my bag, he threatened me, but I told him that I had nothing on me. I even let him check my pockets. My check, un-cashed was in my book bag. My cousin wasn't so lucky. The other boys caught him, pulled out a pair of box cutters, and stole his money. My cousin quit Youth Patrol after that. Finally, I quit shortly after.

Bad things happen all the time. I've seen it. I've experienced it.

But I'm proud to say that I never did anything to hurt other people.

But I have done some pretty stupid things.

When I was about 12 years old, I did what every other kid in my neighborhood liked to do: go up to the roof of the eight-story building. Well, one day, after going up to the roof, I was confronted by a kid who dared me to go back up and jump off….and so I said….

"Okay"

When I reached the top and looked over the fence, I saw a crowd of people looking at me...because he must have told everybody that I was going to jump. So I was trying to figure out a way to get myself mentally prepared for this jump, because I was seriously considering doing this. And then I got this bright idea: I took off my shirt and threw it off the roof... because I wanted to know where I was going to land when I jumped. Apparently I thought I was as light as a shirt. Then I watched the shirt as it landed in a tree...a thorny tree. And that by the way is what convinced me not to jump, not my own death, but some thorns in a tree. I never said I was the brightest kid. Ironically, over two decades later, I'd write about believing that I could fly, but that was obviously metaphorical for the drive we need to succeed, not literal for a desire to prove something to someone at the cost of my own life. And over two decades later, I've learned to joke about that experience, but humor aside, it was a stupid thing to do. I'm glad I came to my senses.

Normally, I did sensible things. Normally, I did things that made me a good kid. But eventually I learned that not only was doing something stupid bad, but also doing what was normal and doing what was good wasn't good enough. It was a lesson I learned in high school that convinced me that in order to succeed in life, you cannot simply focus on not doing the wrong thing, and you cannot just focus on simply doing the right thing, which is the expected thing, you have to do beyond what is expected. We must be motivated, not only by doing the right thing, not only by doing what's expected, but also and most importantly, by what can be gained by doing beyond what is expected.

It was the first class I had ever failed….ever. I never experienced academic failure before. I always worked hard and earned good grades. But in the tenth grade, I was faced with my first academic struggle. I had been such an ace at math since the day Felix challenged me to complete the multiplication table in one night. Math was my passion. When my second grade teacher Mrs. McIntyre challenged us to do long division with four digit numbers, I'd go home and create bigger math problems with longer digits, just to challenge myself. But geometry changed me forever. I won't mention her name because this former teacher always hated when I told this story to students, after I returned to my alma mater as a teacher. It's too bad she felt that way because I tell this story with pride. After one term of struggle, I earned a failing grade in the class. And I had decided that I would confront my teacher. After I squared my shoulders, I simply said, "But I do all my homework." And her response became a motto to adopt and live by: "You're supposed to do your homework." That was all she had to say to make the message clear. There are no brownie points for doing what you are expected to do. Doing what you're expected to do is not enough. From then on, I had begun to go the extra mile. I went the extra mile the very next term when I retook the class. To my dismay, when I walked into the class of a very large high school with over 30 math teachers, I saw her again. What were the odds? I could have requested a transfer. But I didn't. And I consider that one of my greatest decisions. I took her on again, did more than I was expected to do, and I passed. I don't remember my grade, but that doesn't matter. The lesson proved to be critically more important.

I've been an educator for over 17 years. I've taught, coordinated student activities, directed school plays, organized orientations, delivered presentations for parents, taught leadership development, mentored struggling students, chaperoned trips, trained staff, and moved furniture. And I firmly believe that had I not done more than what was expected of me that I would not have ascended to the role of Assistant Principal. So yes, I've broken a sweat and exhausted faculties only to trade more hours for less money. But in the end, I'm better for it. I'm more skilled, more connected, and more primed for future opportunities. And I'm still ready, willing, and able to continue to do more. There's nothing to be gained from doing less. There's nothing gained from doing what you're not supposed to do. There's incredible gain from doing more, from going beyond, from going the extra mile.

She may not want the attention, but I want to thank my 10th grade high school math teacher. We should all take heed to a lesson that not only can add to our development but can multiply our success. (I know that was a cheesy connection between the lesson and the fact that it was taught by my math teacher. Forgive me for being corny.) But once you finish laughing at me, remember these words and then go beyond the expected.

"No one ever attains very eminent success by simply doing what is required of him; it is the amount and excellence of what is over and above the required, that determines the greatness of ultimate distinction. – Charles Francis Adams

"Today, and every day, deliver more than you are getting paid to do. The victory of success will be half won when you learn the secret of putting out more than is expected in all that you do. Make yourself so valuable in your work that eventually you will become indispensable. Exercise your privilege to go the extra mile, and enjoy all the rewards you receive." – Og Mandino

Chapter Seven: Follow Your Guides

"For everyone of us that succeeds, it's because there's somebody there to show you the way out." -Oprah Winfrey

"Most people can do absolutely awe-inspiring things. Sometimes they just need a little nudge." -Timothy Ferriss

Follow the advice of those who have your best interest at heart.

We must be motivated by the fact that we don't always have a full vision of what is best for us.

We have nothing to lose, but always something to gain from guidance.

Being an only child, I am a very independent person. And therefore, I must admit that I struggle with this advice. But experience has taught me that I need to get over it because sometimes others see what you don't see, know what you don't know, and use their vantage point to make you better.

I am so thankful to my cousin Teresa and my Aunt Niameh. When I was in the sixth grade, they took a trip to my school to investigate how I could be switched to a new district for middle school. They were told that I would have to sit for some type of exam. What did I know? I never questioned this. I never rebelled against it. They went out of their way because they believed that staying in my district would not be best for my education and future. So I took the test and passed it. And after graduation, I was off to a middle school outside of my neighborhood. And though I agonized over walking home on rainy days and sitting in classrooms with kids who seemingly were more well off than I was, I think I am a better person because of the transfer. I met new people, was exposed to a new environment, and escaped any distraction that might have steered me down the wrong path. Did they save me? I think the answer lies in my experience at Youth Patrol where one co-worker shared that she hated the job because all of the kids who threatened us or attacked us were the same kids who tortured her and others at school, the same middle school I would have attended had it not been for that transfer.

But I wasn't in the clear yet. Soon, it became time to apply to high school. And though I tried my hardest, I didn't score high enough to be enrolled in any of New York City's specialized high schools. So I went to a school in midtown Manhattan, where I aimed to study media communications. Only a few months in, my aunt Grace urged me to retake the specialized high school exam. She was worried that the Manhattan school was not safe. I guess that's why I never told her about Halloween day. Halloween was always a day to fear as long as I can remember. I only had one positive memory: when I was four years old, my mother took me door-to-door in our small apartment building where I shyly pranced around in my Fred Flinstone costume. The positive memories would not return until I began to take my own children out on the streets of 7th Avenue in Brooklyn to collect treats from the various storeowners. Every Halloween in between is smeared by the scare of people putting razor blades in apples. And then school children would take the day off in fear of being hit with eggs, sprayed with Neet hair removal, or beat up. I always had perfect attendance, despite Halloween. I actually survived 12 years of public school without ever taking off on a Halloween. But this particular Halloween is not a pleasant memory. When I arrived to school, I noticed that attendance was very low. There were no crowds that I had to rush through on my way to first period. When I went to the cafeteria during 5th period, there were only two other kids present. There were usually a couple of hundred. I started to doubt my decision to go to school that day. I saw one friend in the hallway who made me promise to wait for him after school so we could travel home together. So I went to all of my classes. But it was during the last period of the day that I realized how courageous I was to go to school that day. I was the only kid to arrive. Even the teacher asked shockingly, "Why are you here?" I stayed though because I promised my friend that I would wait. One step out of the building, several apples darted pass our heads. Eggs crashed to the floor. Behind us, a gang of boys pounded the pavement in a fierce chase toward us. We ran so unbelievably fast. I don't know how we escaped. We couldn't have been luckier that the train had just pulled in as we leapt onto the platform floor. I never told aunt Grace, my mother, or anyone else for that matter. But I'm sure that aunt Grace knew, not of that experience or even about the first day of school when I was threatened by some kid on the streets of Times Square, but that there were experiences. When I followed her advice and inquired about transferring to a new school, my guidance counselor informed me that I had the highest average in my class. Maybe if I had stayed, I might have earned scholarships, accolades, and all the other benefits reaped by a top scholar. But I took aunt Grace's advice. I took the exam for the specialized high schools. The second time around, I passed the exam. I got into a school that proved to be a life changer. I was no longer the top scholar. I even failed my first class. But I learned to work hard, I spent a lot of time doing extra-curricular activities, and I discovered a passion for public speaking. I never became the valedictorian, but according to Ned Steele, a contributing writer to an alumni magazine, I did become the "Total Technite".

He wrote:

Anything can happen at Brooklyn Tech, and one recent Saturday afternoon, it does. The world's most famous film director, James Cameron ("Titanic" and "Avatar") and movie star Sigourney Weaver occupy the auditorium's grand stage, leading a high-profile student public-speaking competition.

But the celebrity visitors can only watch in admiration as the scene is stolen by an energetic dynamo-in-motion of a man who ignites the crowd, first with a rousing welcome and animated banter and later with his dazzling, inspired talk on injecting Avatar's themes into the classroom.

"You're a rock star," a Cameron colleague shouts out to Marc Williams, Brooklyn Tech alumnus and the school's newest assistant principal.

But the public face of the spirited performer is nowhere to be seen on another early spring afternoon, this one in the cramped seventh-floor assistant principal's office. Here, an anxious parent phones Marc Williams to voice fears that her child will not eat properly on the forthcoming senior trip to Disney World. As the chat morphs into an extended airing of the mother's concerns over the student's college prospects, Mr. Williams listens sympathetically, for longer than he can afford to, then assures the parent her child is solidly on track.

Next, a student strolls in confidently, hoping for permission to begin ticket sales for an upcoming music competition. But Mr. Williams remembers, from the previous year's event, that some participants found the contest rules unfair. He draws the student organizer standing before him into a conversation much deeper than the one she had anticipated.

Finally, a poignant, challenging moment: Another parent calls, requesting a schedule shift for her child to switch from music band to chorus. The student, a freshman, is scoring excellent grades but, early in her high school experience, is generally unhappy. Joining chorus, where the child's talent and passion lie, might do the trick, the parent suggests.

Mr. Williams works the system and presses all the buttons, but logistically the program switch won't work. The child will have to wait until next year.

Mr. Williams delivers the disappointing news with sensitivity and empathy. But he's not finished yet: he promises the mother he will give her child his personal attention, and he points out that the student will likely make new friends as the semester unfolds.

Voice Of Tech

So Marc Williams' day starts at a makeshift broadcast base in the great auditorium's rear orchestra, announcing sports team wins and upcoming activities in a lively, literate four-minute show he scripts nightly at home after his two children are asleep. To the students, it is a refreshing and entertaining break in the day's routine. One day, perhaps after they graduate, they will realize it is much more: a daily, subliminal invitation to widen their horizons.

BEYOND LIMITATIONS

The day progresses to the tight alcove office upstairs, where plaques line the walls with words of gratitude from the classes of 1998, 2000, 2001, 2005, 2008 and 2009. Here, where no one else watches or listens, he turns problems into solutions, reassures distraught parents and guides awkward teenagers to their first glimpses of the road to maturity.

Problem solver

"Marc is the ultimate student advocate, and the conduit for information to parents and the outside world. He personifies the ideal Technite: a problem solver and decision maker, enthusiastic, with an unparalleled work ethic. I wish we could cast a mold and make more of him."

Yet another day at Tech finds Marc Williams facing a tearful mother's anxieties about her child's academic performance. He listens empathetically – for a long time – then delicately helps her to see that the student's behavior is actually typical, and that it might be best all around if she were to consider exerting less parental pressure on the child. Conveying such a nuanced message is a tough balancing act, but he pulls it off superbly, in the eyes of parent coordinator.

"Marc has years and years of insights into teenagers," she says. "He resolves issues in a way that is very caring. He is the heart and soul of Tech."

So much of what I have accomplished in life can be attributed to the education and experience I received as a Brooklyn Tech student and as a Brooklyn Tech teacher-turned-administrator. Brooklyn Tech has been a life-changing experience. And yet, it would not have ever had an impact on me had it not been for my aunt Grace leading me to that path. Somehow, aunt Grace knew. And I'm so glad that I listened to her. My future changed drastically simply because I was willing to follow her guidance.

And I tell you what else Aunt Grace knew. She knew that it would have been a mistake to take a year or more off during college.

BEYOND LIMITATIONS

After my first year at NYU, I was faced with an unfortunate reality. I couldn't afford the tuition. Maybe I should have gone to a CUNY school where I would have been eligible for full financial aid. And maybe Aunt Grace could have suggested that I just transfer, but she was too distracted by the horror of what I said to her on the phone as I sunk down the hall after receiving the bill from the Bursar's Office:

"Aunt Grace, I think I'm going to have to take a year from school. It costs too much money."

She begged me to not to do it. She desperately asked if there was anything I could do.

"Can't you take out a loan?"

I had taken out a loan for the first year of school. I had qualified for the Perkins Loan. But, admittedly, I did not pay attention to the deadlines and guidelines of the Perkins Loan. I didn't reapply when I was supposed to; so I was not eligible for the second year. After some further inquiry, I was told that I could apply for a Stafford Loan. So that's what I did. I'm still repaying that loan. But if I wasn't in this position of repaying a student loan, I might be in a mess much worse. Staying in school, staying on track with my education was critical. I believe that it contributed to the butterfly effect that led me to a career in education and back to my alma mater where I hope I have contributed and continue to contribute to the elevation of another generation.

Somehow Aunt Grace knew

And somehow Theresa and Aunt Niameh knew.

Sometimes, you never know where the guidance of others may lead you. Sometimes, you can be steered in the wrong direction, but that usually doesn't happen when you follow those who clearly and undoubtedly have your best interest in their hearts and minds. Success is not only the result of your vision, but also the result of the guiding eyes of others who have been where you have been, who have achieved what you are trying to do, or who see the potential you can meet and exceed.

You can look in the mirror, but you still can't see yourself.

BEYOND LIMITATIONS

You can look ahead, but you can't see from afar.

We all have people in our lives who have the view, the knowledge, the experience. We have to be willing to listen, to follow. When I have the opportunity to do so, I try to be a source of guidance, a mentor. That's why I visited a high school in Staten Island, New York, to help my former drama teacher and her principal provide guidance for their freshman class. That's why I took the opportunity to speak to an audience of adults at a Hire Fair in Brooklyn, New York. I have to do this because I am better because of the guidance of my family, my friends, and my mentors.

So allow yourself to be led when necessary. Find yourself a mentor. Take the advice given to you. Those who have our best interest at heart will guide us in the right direction. They may not get us to our destination because that's still our responsibility, but they will help us get there.

"Listen to advice and accept correction, then in the end you will be wise." - Anonymous

"To accept good advice is but to increase one's own ability"

-Johann Wolfgang von Goethe

Chapter Eight: Talk Positive

"I found that when you start thinking and saying what you really want then your mind automatically shifts and pulls you in that direction. And sometimes it can be that simple, just a little twist in vocabulary that illustrates your attitude and philosophy." –Jim Rohn

The most incredible thing that separates us from all other animals in existence is our minds. Our minds not only have the power to provoke thought, but also to create action. And remember, it is our thoughts that lead to action. And the only way inaction occurs or actions that are not in out best interest occur is when we feed poisonous thoughts into our minds.

Negativity is the homicide of all dreams.
Don't kill the dream.
Create it. Nurture it. Feed it.
Feed it with Positivity.

I say we should all go on a diet. Our world is often obsessed with our physical appearance, so much so that the fitness business and the fitness craze are at an unbelievable high. But if we could match the intensity of those physical workouts and diet plans with an exercise and a diet for the mind and become obsessed with strengthening our mental capabilities, then the possibilities are endless.

True strength lies in our mentality.
Feed the mind.
Conquer the world.

My wife admitted to me the other day that she has a secret to how she was able to reform her fit physique after three pregnancies that took place over the course of five years. She was always into working out. She was always into eating healthy. But one's body after pregnancy seems to present a physical and psychological challenge to the desirable body most

BEYOND LIMITATIONS

women want. My wife had been a member of a local Weight Watcher's Club for the longest time. So she was familiar with the plan and the strategies that could help her get back the body she craved. So one morning after our third child Dylan was born, Lauren pushed herself to attend a Saturday morning Weight Watchers meeting. The weigh-in was the same. The pamphlets were the same. The goal was the same. But something different occurred that morning, something that Lauren had not experienced at any other club meeting before: it was the words of the guest speaker. This speaker moved the audience. She reignited their purpose. She inspired their personal mission. She motivated them towards achievement. Lauren said it was that speech that worked the most. And she looks good!

A former student once said to me, about the English language in particular, though it can be applied to all languages, "It's amazing that all we have are 26 letters and yet the vast combinations of those letters possess unbelievable power." But it is all language, both spoken and non-verbal, that possesses amazing power. And our potential to do anything, in response to the language we choose to speak and the language we choose to listen to, is limitless.

After delivering a presentation to an audience of parents and students about effective study habits, one parent approached me with a question for his college-bound son: he wanted to know how does one "stay motivated". It was a great question that addresses the everyday struggle that can only be resolved by a daily discussion. Yes, I suggested to him that what we need on a daily basis is a daily discussion with ourselves. We have to make it a habit to do what I like to call the P.E.P. T.A.L.K.

P.E.P.

Positivity Exudes Productivity

It is my firm belief that the road to success and achievement is optimism. I still have memories of the time when my aunt Niameh registered my mother for a Literacy program at the Brooklyn Public Library. I remember thinking, that as noble of a gesture as that was, at the age of 50+, and after a lifetime of not being able to read or write, how realistic was it that my mother was going to be able to read or write after a few sessions in a literacy class. Nevertheless, I watched my mother make the effort. She would attend the classes on Eastern Parkway. She would bring back homework. One night, I tried to help her with her homework…it was my first experience as a teacher…I clearly did not possess the patience that I would later need in my own classrooms. Teaching my mother how to write her own name was frustrating for me. Teaching my mother how to learn the sequence of the ten buttons on the telephone so that she could call aunt Grace was so frustrating. It's amazing how frustrating it can be to teach something that comes so easily to you but is difficult for others. I keep that in mind every time I mentor a young student who just doesn't believe that he is smart, who doesn't believe that he can do the work, who doesn't believe he'll ever make anything of himself, and that there is no use because he just doesn't know how to be positive. I've learned to fight that frustration with patience. With patience comes positivity. We can allow ourselves to slow down our thought process and not to think and react impulsively. Frustration is impulsive. Patience is strategic. So I told myself that it was possible for her to learn something, despite the challenges. I learned many years later, way after my mother passed, that she had not made it past an elementary school education. So this was a struggle and a challenge, maybe even a nearly impossible task. And yet, because she would try, because she would stay positive, she was able to take that long bus ride to the library on Eastern Parkway, and sit by my side at the last session to hear her name called as she received her Certificate of Completion. She never was able to write much after those classes. As a matter of fact, all she was able to write was…

J-O-H-A-N-N-A

…but that was more than I had ever seen her write in my life…it was a step beyond writing an "X" on the signature line. I was the proudest son. And I was a son who learned through his own mother's struggle, positivity, and effort that if you maintain a positive attitude, you can push yourself to accomplishment…and maybe even beyond.

BEYOND LIMITATIONS

"If you will call your troubles experiences, and remember that every experience develops some latent force within you, you will grow vigorous and happy, however adverse your circumstances may seem to be." – John Heywood

"Having a positive mental attitude is asking how something can be done rather than saying it can't be done." –Bo Bennett

"Few things in the world are more powerful than a positive push. A smile. A word of optimism and hope. And you can do it when things are tough." –Richard M. DeVos

Consider everything that occurred during the Civil Rights movement in America. How could all of that pain and tragedy not drain the thousands of hopefuls, including one Dr. Martin Luther King Jr.? He believed. He believed that one day things would be different. And while one could argue that racism exists to this day, one cannot argue that the status quo is a whole lot better than the stories history has told. Progress was the product of a positive attitude. The belief that one day life would be better was all it took to keep going. Positivity is Productivity. Positivity has given many the power to be proactive, to be progressive, to be productive.

I read an article about brain research that stated that whenever something makes us angry, frustrated, or stressed, there's an impulse in our brain that puts us in attack mode. That same research shows that the intensity of that impulse decreases after approximately ten seconds. That's why it is often recommended that we step back, breathe, and count to ten. But I say that instead of counting to ten, we should self-talk. And as we choose to show self-control during those seconds of intense emotions, we should choose our verbal and non-verbal language strategically to help us achieve a desired outcome.

****

BEYOND LIMITATIONS

The P.E.P. T.A.L.K.

Tell yourself positive things

There was a time when I fell so far behind in my student loan payments that I received a call from an agency stating that my wages would be garnished. And despite my pleas, there was nothing I could say or even do to prevent the inevitable. I hung up the phone and tried my best to hold in the tears; the tears of feeling helpless, overwhelmed, and defeated dragged down my face, but it didn't take long to take a deep breathe and say to myself, "When nothing works in your favor and frustration and disappointment make you want to quit. Don't do it. Find a way. Because there is a way."

I remember mentoring one kid who lost her drive to do anything. She just didn't think she had it in her anymore to be positive, to do anything with her life. And regardless of whom she talked to and all the uplifting advice we all tried to give her, nothing seemed to get her out of this slump. One day, I asked her to role-play a conversation with her former and current self, between her motivated, happy self and her unmotivated, depressed persona. What she scripted was a self-therapy session that had a profound effect on her mood. It turned out that even though she told herself the same things that many of us had told her, the words had more impact coming from her own inner voice.

Research shows that the act of giving ourselves mental messages can help us learn and perform at our best. And as Aaron Weintraub wrote in *"Great Self-Talk: How Elite Athletes Coach Themselves"*, *"A positive attitude and positively worded self-talk affect behavior more than many people realize because of the nature of the mind-body connection."* Weintraub's article is about how athletes use self-talk to achieve their peak performance. And no athlete self-talked any better than the great Michael Jordan on the night of June 11, 1997 when the Chicago Bulls faced the Utah Jazz in the NBA Playoffs, in a contest that will forever be etched in the annuls of time as ""The Flu Game".

BEYOND LIMITATIONS

Sportswriter Rick Weinberg wrote for ESPN25, *"It's 4:30 p.m. when Scottie Pippen sees Jordan emerge from a side door of the Delta Center. 'The way he looked, there's no way I thought he could even put on his uniform,' Pippen would say. 'I'd never seen him like that. He looked bad -- I mean really bad.' Jordan sequesters himself in a dark room adjacent to the Bulls' locker room. He slowly lies his weak body down. He closes his eyes. He visualizes himself running, shooting, passing, rebounding, dunking. Soon, he emerges from the room, staggering slowly. He puts on his uniform and walks out to the court, weak and pale. 'I can play,' he tells coach Phil Jackson. As the game begins, Jordan drags himself up and down the court, running at only 65 percent of his normal speed. He is so dehydrated and fatigued that he is sure he is going to pass out any second. Halfway through the quarter, during a pause in the game, Jordan bends over to rest, pulls on his shorts, closes his eyes and nearly falls over. He has no energy whatsoever. 'In the third quarter, I felt like I couldn't catch my wind and get my energy level up,' Jordan would say later. 'I don't know how I got through the fourth quarter. I was just trying to gut myself through it. That was probably the most difficult thing I've ever done,' he would say after the game. 'I almost played myself into passing out just to win a basketball game. If we had lost, I would have been devastated.' Jackson was almost at a loss for words, but finally told the media, 'Because of the circumstances, with this being a critical game in the Finals, I'd have to say this is the greatest game I've seen Michael play. Just standing up was nauseating for him and caused him dizzy spells. This was a heroic effort, one to add to the collection of efforts that make up his legend." After MJ's epic performance, Pippen would say, "He's the greatest, and everyone saw why tonight.'"*

So how did he do it? Almost all, if not all of us, have had the flu. We know how difficult it is to do just the simplest of tasks when the flu consumes us. I've felt like the walking dead. Just the thought of getting out of bed is a physical and psychological challenge. And the thought of doing anything like playing a basketball game, let alone trying to win a game is unthinkable. But he did just that. But how? The medical personnel said that there was no way he would be able to play Game 5.

BEYOND LIMITATIONS

His body was too weak.
But his mind was unbelievably focused.
He told the coach…he told himself, "I can play."
The power of our thoughts can empower our abilities.

I often joke with my wife that on a daily basis, I feel like I am 210% and when I'm sick, that's when I feel like I'm only 100%. She laughs and rolls her eyes, but she understands my point: that I always feel that I can always go above and beyond to achieve, regardless of the challenge. I'm sure that's similar to, if not the same as Michael Jordan's positive thought process, the thought process of a champion. And by no means am I comparing my status to that of Michael Jordan's. I can only claim to be "like Marc", but I do have a champion's mentality. And we all can possess that champion's mentality as well. All we have to do is tell ourselves positive things.

That also reminds me of another basketball reference. It was during the 2013 NBA Playoffs. The Miami Heat was competing in Game 6 against the Indiana Pacers. Going into the third quarter, the Heat was down by four points when Lebron James ripped into his teammates a profanity-laced pep talk. The language may have been harsh, but the intent was meant to have a positive impact. And it worked. The Heat transformed a four-point deficit into a thirteen-point lead.

Grant Hughes wrote, for the Bleacher Report, *"And while his individual takeover will get the headlines, James' vocal leadership helped empower his teammates to come along for the ride. Udonis Haslem responded to James' profanity-laced tirade by burying jumpers (he finished 8-of-9 on the night) and playing with the kind of physicality that Miami has lacked against the bigger, stronger Pacers…when he ripped into the Heat in the huddle before taking the floor for the third quarter, James showed that he's also capable of motivating and leading with his words."*

It's amazing how the power of a positive message can empower our potential and our capabilities.

69

BEYOND LIMITATIONS

I was never an athletic coach, but I had some experience as an advisor for a few performance groups at my school. We called the event SING. Three teams created their own original 35-minute musical comedies. An array of judges with criteria and ballots in hand would determine which team produced and performed the best show. I was an advisor for nine SING competitions, with a record of six first place victories. I had the fortune of working with some of the most talented kids. And I give them all the credit in the world for the work they created and their work on the stage. But I will graciously accept the best compliment those kids could have ever bestowed upon me: each time, minutes before stepping out of the dressing room before stepping onto the stage, my kids would ask me to give one of my speeches, because it would fire them up and make them feel like they could take on the world. I wish I would have recorded those speeches, but even though there is no transcript for any of those nine speeches, my memory serves me well enough to remember that my message was the same each and every time: that those kids had what it took to win, and all they had to do was go on to that stage and take it; I believed in them, and most importantly, I wanted them to believe in themselves; I wanted them to believe that they could win. And yes, there were years when they were the youngest group with the least experience, and there were years when the other teams were equally talented and the chance of winning would come down to the difference of one or two points on a single judge's score sheet; nevertheless, I wanted to tell them something positive.

Going back to the sports reference, Thomas H. Giedgowd wrote an article called "The Home Court Advantage in Contempoary College Basketball". He discussed a study of team performance that was conducted by Barry Schwartz and Stephen Barsky. Their study closely analyzed the quality of play of Big Five college basketball teams when they played at home. Schwartz and Barsky found that home teams take more shots and score more field goals and points than they do playing in front of a hostile crowd. They also found that there were no important differences with regard to assists, teamwork, personal fouls, or scores as a percentage of shots, but the Big Five teams did have a distinct advantage when it came to rebounding on their home courts. A study conducted by Phillip E. Varca done on the home crowd advantage in basketball also found that home teams play more aggressively at home, and exhibit more aggressive tendencies when playing in front of a friendly crowd. Most of us have participated in the home crowd cheers. We know the positive, motivational chants we scream towards our favorite teams. Those cheers don't always result in a win. But how many of us have seen those games or the movies about games when the team we were rooting for does win in the end? It's inspirational isn't it? It's just evident that the mind is such a sponge of inspiration. All we need to do is to send messages to the mind; all we need to do is be our own mental cheerleaders.

I think this point about telling ourselves, or for that matter telling others, positive things is best summarized by a statement I heard while watching a special about pop artist Will.i.am. When asked about how he dealt with the constant rejections, as he and the Black Eyed Peas pursued their music career, he said that he decided a long time ago that "No" does not mean "no, but rather that "No" means "to know" the parameters and to learn from them so that we can use that "know"ledge to progress and achieve. That's a positive spin if I've ever heard one.

What we choose to say to ourselves is key to accomplishing our desired goals. They are key to the momentum we need on a daily basis to resist the daily temptation to do anything else but the work we need to do to accomplish the things we desire.

"Please remember that sometimes the diet we need to be on is a spiritual and emotional one. Be cautious with what you feed your mind and soul. Fuel yourself with positivity and let that fuel propel you into positive action." -Steve Maraboli

****

BEYOND LIMITATIONS

The P.E.P. T.A.L.K
Act in a Positive Manner

I remember being in the fifth grade when my teacher selected me to be a member of the Color Guard. I was a flag bearer. I held the American Flag. I was so proud. And as I stood in the back of the auditorium, flagpole in hand, shoulders squared, back straight, legs sturdy, and feet planted firmly on the ground, prepared for a power march to the center of the stage, I felt the confidence build within my body. The nerves slipped away. I felt like I was on top of the world. I recently read several articles about the power of the pose and the power of good posture. And I learned that studies show that we can actually change our mood by simply changing the way we stand or sit.

I remember drudging uphill with the stroller, my two youngest children in tow, on a hot, sweltering day. My nerves hit a high as close as the temperature. The frustration was building as my muscles became tense, the sweat became heavy, and the thoughts of "Why can't these kids just walk! I'm tired of pushing this damn stroller everywhere!" clouded my mind. And as I caught myself self-talking negative and slouching over as I pushed forward, I decided to straighten my back, power up my legs, loosen the muscles between my brows, and smile.

I decided to change my body language.

And with that gesture, I made a conscious decision to change my mood. And that's what I did....I changed my mood.

How we carry ourselves can actually change our mood, which greatly affects how we approach situations and solve problems. Studies show that repositioning ourselves to an upright, positive position can change our mood and make us feel better. And social-science research indicates that a power stance or position releases a flood of hormones that can make us feel more positive. Dana Carney, a social psychologist at the Haas School of Business at the University of California said that the hormonal changes that occur during a power pose could start a physiological cascade that lasts all day. In other words, research shows that good posture not only reflects our mood, but most importantly, it affects our mood. So whenever we feel anxious, nervous, stressed, or negative, the positive thing to do is to take that "Superman" pose. Sit up straight and stand tall. That's how we create that positive energy.

It's really all about catching yourself before allowing the anger, the stress, or the frustration from getting in the way. Once those emotions settle in, we are detoured in a direction that is far from rising above and beyond.

I'm reminded again of my children. Don't get me wrong...I love them more than the world itself...remember they are the reason why I do what I do...but there are those moments. On several occasions while walking my two oldest to school, I have found myself stressed by the simultaneous conversations, or as I like to call them the calls for attention; stressed by the slow pace, trailing on the heels of running late; stressed by the balancing act of an umbrella in the pouring rain, two hands I must hold while crossing the street, and the two different book bags sliding off my shoulders as my foot sinks into a large river of rainwater.

Stressed is an accurate word.
But equally accurate is the word "tense".

Science shows that stress and tension are nearly one in the same because as we feel emotionally stressed, we feel physically tense.

I began to notice where the tension in my body lied the strongest as I struggled with the stress of the early morning drop-offs; the tension collapsed between my brows, in the center of my forehead, the land of the migraine headaches. One day, it dawned on me to consciously loosen and expand the muscles in that space and then force myself to smile. Fake smiles work too by the way because the brain doesn't actually know the difference.

Each morning I tried that.
And each morning, it worked better.

BEYOND LIMITATIONS

In an article titled "Muscle Tension", author Eric Harrison wrote, "Scanning the body carefully brings out hidden tensions to the surface. It allows us to relax those muscles that are within our conscious control, and encourages those that we can't control to relax in their own time. When we supply the brain with information about where the muscles are contracting due to stress, we help our brains make the necessary adjustments to remedy the situation."

Researchers call it isometric tension. When we get angry, frustrated, stressed, and negative, the muscles in our bodies tend to contract, which is what causes that tension. The contraction of those muscles then impedes the flow of blood and oxygen. And then it creates tension in other parts of the body. Researchers explain that our bodies react this way to prepare us for some type of confrontation.

Eric Harrison also stated, "A stress response starts in the emotional brain. The amygdala detects a problem and initiates the contraction of big and small muscles throughout the body. This 'coiled spring' feeling is called 'a preparatory set'. The body is setting itself up in preparation for action by tensing the muscles appropriate to that task."

And sometimes that might be necessary when you have to defend yourself and counterattack. But in many other cases, that's not the best course of action. Imagine if I had done that. What kind of father would I be if I rose my hand to strike my kids just because they were both trying to have a conversation with me, walking at a child's pace, trying to escape the rain, while looking forward to going to, of all places, school. I would have been a real jerk who had no self-control. That would have been uncalled for, cruel, counterproductive, and counter-positive. Now, I catch myself more often then I used to. Even the other day as the whole family took a neighborhood walk, my oldest fell to the ground and barely scraped his knee. He screamed for nearly 20 minutes. A stranger would have thought that he had torn an ACL. And then my little girl interrupted me, not only to complain about the sun that was shining in her eyes, but also to show me where she had cut her foot two weeks ago. I responded, "Don't take your shoe off right now." I didn't want her to put her barefoot on the sidewalk. That was enough to set her off. Her sensitivity threshold is about as low as my oldest son's threshold for pain. Picture the four and six year-olds screaming in tears while being chauffeured in the double stroller, while the two year old walks calmly uphill, as I anticipated a third meltdown.

In one second, I caught myself saying, "I can't..."

And then I stopped myself and changed my language..."I can. I can handle this." I then squared my shoulders, straightened my back, loosened and expanded the muscles in my forehead, smiled, and power-walked up the hill.

I'm not saying it's easy to stop yourself and consciously decide to speak and act positive. It surely takes work, and to be redundant, a conscious effort, but we do have that control. We need to have it. And we need to exercise it as often as we can. We will slip sometimes, but we want to slip less and decrease the likelihood of negative consequences.

Unfortunately, I can think of a few examples of people who lost their cool during a heightened moment of tension and as a result lost a lot more than they had expected. Michael Richards embodied one of the most iconic characters in television history: Kramer, from the show Seinfeld. And yet, his most notable experience that impeded what potentially could have been an increasingly successful career was the infamous night at a comedy club when he lashed out at a heckler. His career has never been the same. And then there's Chris Brown. While he has been fortunate enough to bounce back from a most infamous tragic meltdown involving Rihanna, he will forever live with the judgment of the public about how he managed the tension of that moment. His inability to act in a positive manner in that single instance nearly cost him his career and most definitely had a negative impact on his financial growth and success. Now I'm not here to judge these men or any one else who has from time to time lost the battle to isometric tension. Hell, I've lost that battle sometimes myself. I just want to point out that there can be some negative consequences when we don't take control and make the conscious decision to act in a positive manner.

BEYOND LIMITATIONS

Some experts suggest meditation. Some suggest yoga. Some suggest breathing exercises. But whatever your mode of tension release is, remember that we can easily do something to soothe the contraction of those muscles, and not only does the entire body benefit if we do, but whatever we hope to accomplish increases exponentially.

Now the third essential positive action is something that we're all capable of doing and yet it is said that this action requires 40% of our facial muscles to do: smile. I once mentored a former student who looked so depressed as he sat across from me, mulling over a future that seemed to have no prospects because the past few months had dragged him into a downward spiral from which he felt he could not escape. After we talked about his struggles and obstacles, and identified a few plans of action, I brought to his attention his demeanor. I told him that our physiology plays such an important role in our mood and our ability to be increasingly productive. I told him that he needed to find his smile. I may have not said it in such a cheesy fashion, but that was my message. I shared with him the study about the yearbook photos: that a greater percentage of those who smiled in their photos have achieved a greater level of success later in life compared to their classmates who did not flash a smile.

One article I read stated, *"studies have shown that people who smile frequently and are friendlier towards their clients and customers earn higher tips and make more sales. People who look confident and capable, because that's the message smiling constantly communicates to others, are also more likely to be asked to take on important leadership tasks."* (http://roomofmyown.hubpages.com/hub/The-Social-Emotional-and-Financial-Benefits-of-Smiling)

Research also shows that smiling increases our energy levels which means it increases our productivity levels, giving us the boost we need to "power through the day". Furthermore, smiling releases endorphins and reduces the cortisol in our bodies and in turn, drives away negative feelings.

BEYOND LIMITATIONS

The next time I met with that mentee, he appeared to be much happier, flashing smiles and enjoying laughs. His future had brightened. He said he was happier because of the changes he made to restart his journey to what he aims to accomplish. And I'm sure that is true, but the slump of negativity, frustration, or depression can be turned upside down when we consciously change the way we work those facial muscles, contorting them into a smile. Smiling is not just the result of things going our way. Smiling has proven to be the catalyst for moving forward. Studies show that when we exercise those facial muscles to frown or to pout, our ability to focus narrows. Notice that when we get upset, we struggle to think about anything else. And as a result, we become stuck and stagnant, unproductive, and counter-positive. Research shows that smiling creates calmness and then that relaxed state *"increases our ability to notice fine details, see problems from a new perspective and find creative solutions" that we might otherwise miss when we're pissed off.* ((http://roomofmyown.hubpages.com/hub/The-Social-Emotional-and-Financial-Benefits-of-Smiling)

It's amazing how the power of our non-verbal, intrapersonal communication can empower us to rise beyond our struggles and enable us to do positive and productive things.

"There's gon' be some stuff you gon' see that's gon' make it hard to smile in the future. But through whatever you see, through all the rain and the pain, you gotta keep your sense of humor. You gotta be able to smile" -Tupac and Scarface

****

BEYOND LIMITATIONS

The P.E.P. T.A.L.K.
Listen to and read positive messages

While this is similar to telling ourselves positive things, it's a little different and absolutely necessary. When we find ourselves consumed with frustration, anger, and stress, and we can't seem to think about anything else, we often need another source of inspiration, motivation, and positivity to lift our spirits, to help us climb out of that metaphorical hole, and to push us forward. And even when we aren't consumed by these negative emotions, we sometimes find ourselves so accustomed to the routine sounds and language of our own inner voice of motivation that our words lose a little of their steam; so we can use another source of motivation, inspiration, positivity to reenergize ourselves pass the point of exhaustion or stagnation.

Sometimes we need a new voice, a new vocabulary, a new set of metaphors, and a new language. Sometimes, when we struggle to think positive because the struggle and frustration is just too much, the words we find in a book or on a recording have proven to do the trick. Norman Doidge M.D. states that the brain has the capacity to rewire itself and/or form new neural pathways. All that is required is a repetitive activity like reading and listening to positive messages to reinforce new learning. In addition, Andrew Newberg, M.D. and Mark Robert Waldman wrote, in their article *"Words Can Change Your Brain"*, *"To overcome a neural bias for negativity, we must repetitiously and consciously generate as many positive thoughts as we can. Barbara Fredrickson, one of the founders of Positive Psychology, discovered that we need to generate at least three positive thoughts and feelings for each expression of negativity. If you express fewer than three, personal and business relationships are likely to fail."* What that means to me is that our positive thoughts alone may not be enough. They have to be reinforced and repeated over and over again. That's why we need to listen and read positive messages as well.

While in high school, I would go to a local poster store, when hanging posters in your bedroom was still popular. And among the many posters of celebrities I would purchase, I also started to collect those

BEYOND LIMITATIONS

scenic posters with the inspirational quotes. When I became a teacher, I would hang those types of posters all over the classroom. And yet, I never read anything lengthier than a quote, not until recently in fact. And now that I have compiled a library of motivational advice and positive messages, I have found that my positive spirit and my drive are even stronger. I've taken to the bookstore. I've taken to Twitter. I've taken to the Internet. And I've even taken to writing messages for others to read.

Many months ago, I wrote the following message on a social media site:

"We all struggle with something. And the worst part about any struggle we face is that struggles have the power to wear away at our drive and motivation. Sometimes we feel so defeated that we want to quit. We wonder why we're being punished. Why are we so unlucky? But that's when we have to dig deepest and find that inner strength to keep fighting. Because struggle is not about being unlucky or being punished. It's about developing a strength that will build the fire from the ashes.

So don't fall victim to the struggle.

Embrace the struggle.

And then rise above it. Because you can."

A friend of mine responded, ""Kind of needed to read this right now."

And there are countless other testimonials from celebrities and highly successful people who testify to the impact of the words written in books by Stephen Covey, Dale Carnegie, Napolean Hill, Tony Robbins, Brian Tracy, John Maxwell, Les Brown, and others. There are hundreds of motivational books, thousands of motivational websites, thousands of motivational seminars, and thousands of audio recordings, all authored by motivational speakers, peak performance coaches, and life coaches. They all serve as fuel and kindle for that fire. That's why I spent several months composing blogs on my website and speeches for several audiences that were meant to "boost" others and myself, that were meant to "inspire" others and myself, that were meant to "motivate" others and myself. And I'd like to expand your library with words you can turn to anytime you're in search of a message that can elevate your spirits and give you the boost you need to rise beyond.

I hope these compositions are like that song you might play on your i-pod right before you hit the treadmill at the gym, the same type of song that Michael Phelps listened to right before he hit the water to win his 19th medal, making him the greatest Olympian of all time, the same type of song Lebron James played right before he hit the court to win his first NBA championship. I hope these positive thoughts are like the final scenes in any of those Rocky movies that made you want to hit the floor and do push-ups, race to Philly and hit the stairs of that library, and feel like you could take on the world.

Consider this a dose of positivity, motivation, and inspiration.

BEYOND LIMITATIONS

Quote: "Do what you love; love what you do. Do what you love and you'll never work a day in your life."

Several months ago, a student stopped me in the hall and asked, "Mr. Williams, why are you always smiling? Why are you always so happy? Why do you always say on the loud speaker, 'Have a Safe, Pleasant, and Positive Day?" Okay, she didn't say all of that, but she did ask me why I'm always so happy.

The truth is, I don't remember what I said to her because what I said was so trite and meaningless. I always talk about how much I love teaching. I always talk about seizing the teachable moment. But I didn't seize that moment to teach.

What I should have said is that I'm not always happy because no one is happy 100% of the time. But every time she sees me, I'm at work, doing what I love. I love teaching at one of the best schools in the country. I love being surrounded by the best kids ever. I love creating happy moments, like bringing in celebrities for graduations, proms, and assemblies. I love counseling and giving advice to young people. I love teaching at my old high school where I can give back what was given to me. I love teaching in the classroom, where I can use Michael Jackson's "The Way You Make Me Feel" to teach iambic pentameter, where I can mimic Angelina Jolie as I teach the classic text *Beowulf*, and where I can tell shameful stores about myself to achieve a learning objective. I can inform and entertain at the same time. I can impart knowledge and speak in public all at the same time (Speak in Public…hmmmmm). I love being a teacher. That's why I'm "always happy."

And yet, several months ago, I found myself sitting on my living room floor, intensely taking notes from a DVD series about becoming a paid professional speaker. Then, I began surfing the Internet, looking for opportunities to speak in public, how much a public speaker could be paid, and how to start a career in public speaking. I joined Toastmasters International. I created my website. I started exploring topics that I could write about in a book that would make me the kind of expert that people would hire to speak in public.

BEYOND LIMITATIONS

With that said, one might say that I can't love teaching that much. Nothing could be further from the truth. I have two passions and I have taken the initiative to explore both of them. Actually, I have one passion, to teach. And becoming a professional speaker is my way of increasing the size of my proverbial classroom. So many people never get to do what they love to do because they get sidetracked. They don't do what they want to do because either:

- They HAVE to do something else; (I can accept the realities of life. Sometimes we have to put things on the back burner so that we can do what's practical. But remember that putting your passion on the back burner just means that something else needs your immediate attention. There will be a time when you can bring it back to the front. Just don't forget that the water is boiling on the back burner. Or else, the pot will burn and you'll end up throwing that project in the trash. That's what we call regrets).

- They haven't explored how to transform their passion into a career; (Can you believe that people have paid $500 a ticket to listen to a professional speaker? I found that out while doing research. I can be one of those professional speakers. I just have to learn how. There are so many webpages, so many books, and so many videos about so many people who have found success and happiness doing what they love to do. At 1am, one morning, I found myself listening to a 60-minute radio spot about how one guy discovered his passion, followed his dream, and makes a lucrative living doing what he loves. He shared his tips. I took my notes. The information is out there. The inspiration is out there. You just have to take the initiative to start your search).

- They have been discouraged by other people; (We are the victims of discouraging words because there exists in all of us a fear of failure. I read recently that you should never share your intentions with anyone until you have achieved a small step of success. My goal this summer was to start a website. I didn't tell anyone about my project. When I finished it, I felt a great sense of pride. I then shared it with all the people I know. I don't know for sure what they would have said to me beforehand, but I do know that they've shared many words of encouragement afterwards. Be your own cheerleader while you pursue your passion. You can send the press release once you've achieved some success). By the way, one night I was at a networking event where one young lady surprised her father with the news that for the past several months she had been building her own fashion career with a clothing line. He seemed upset that she never told him. Then I shared with him this thought that often it is best for people to begin the pursuit of their dream before they share their ventures with anyone else so that they can avoid any words of discouragement. That didn't seem to sit well with him. And I guess as a father myself, I would want my children to feel comfortable enough to tell me about their endeavors. I think I am, just like I'm sure that father feels he is, someone that others can share their goals with because I aim to be a cheerleader for the people in my life who are trying to be champions. So if you do have a genuine cheerleader in your life with whom you want to share your goals with, then that's great. Remember, my point is some people get discouraged by the words of other people, but if you don't have that concern, then by all means share and reap the rewards of being encouraged.

- They get impatient because what they want to do could take a long time to achieve; (Not only are we victims of discouraging words, but we are also victims of time. We want instant gratification even though we know it really doesn't exist. That's why weight loss is so difficult. We want the gut to disappear after doing just ten sit-ups. But it just doesn't work that way. I recently read that it could take ten years to experience success as a professional speaker. Ten years is worth the wait, because waiting a lifetime is just the end result of never pursuing a passion.)

There's a new fire in me. I am extremely excited about exploring this field. Where this road will lead, only time will tell. I'm just happy that I'm making the effort.

Have you ever researched what you love to do? Have you ever discovered that there are people who have taken what you love to do and have made a living doing it?

That's the essence of the quote, "Do what you love; love what you do. Do what you love and you'll never work a day in your life": Love. I know it's all semantics when we talk about what we do: a job is nothing but work; a career is just a 9 to 5. But if you focus on the "what you do" part of the quote, then you will "lose focus". But when you are driven by what "you love" to do, then you will find that people are often asking you, "Why are you always so happy?"

It's all about the passion. Explore your passion. Research your passion. Pursue your Passion. Work your Passion. Live your Passion.

Otherwise, you'll just find yourself doing "whatever".

BEYOND LIMITATIONS

Quote: "Hope is not a strategy and luck is not a factor."

One day at the office, I received a call from Disney. They were in the midst of a major promotional campaign for High School Musical 3. My students were trying to win a HSM3 contest to send 300 seniors to DisneyWorld and win a concert featuring Natasha Bedingfield. Disney announced that my school was close to winning the contest. We were the number one school in New York City. And a local morning news show wanted to feature our school's spirited attempt to win this contest. It would be a live video feed! The catch: I had to get hundreds of students to come to school at 5:30am. I did it. It was a memorable experience. There's footage on YouTube.

I was so excited for my students. I was excited for myself. It was an opportunity to create excitement for my entire school and it was an opportunity to host an event for live television.

I love public speaking. I've been told that I have a talent. But the truth is that talent can only take you so far.

What do people need? Drive!

I stood on that stage and ignited the crowd. When my moment came to say something on live TV, I was electric. I was hoping that someone would notice....someone from the local media staff would notice me. I was hoping that after they noticed my talent, someone would offer me an opportunity. The reporter praised me. But then it was over.

It was a brief moment I'll never forget. I was hoping that it would have been so much more.

I came to realize that my problem is that I've always waited for opportunities to present themselves only to hope that they lead to something bigger.

Waiting for something to happen is not a strategy.

Hoping something will happen is not a strategy.

Being lucky that an opportunity presents itself is not a strategy.

BEYOND LIMITATIONS

Do you want to succeed? Then define your specific goal, devise your strategy, and then put your plan into action. Devise a strategy and create your own opportunities.

Creating my website, speaking at national conventions, and writing a book were major steps in my strategy to become a successful professional speaker.

I'm done with hoping.

I'm done with luck.

It's time for a strategy. It's time to put in the work to make things happen.

BEYOND LIMITATIONS

Quote: "What we perceive as our limitations are often only mental obstacles."

She obviously didn't get it. She asked me (with a smirk), "So you think you can fly?" No, I don't think I can fly. But when I told an old friend of mine that I believe that I can do anything, what I meant was that I think there isn't anything I can't do. "What we perceive as our limitations are often only mental obstacles." I know that we all have "human" limitations, but our aspirations and the actions required to achieve our goals have no insurmountable limits, other than the ones we create in our own minds. There are many obstacles in life. There are many roadblocks. There are many forces and factors that exist. That's all true. But the way I see it, we are all capable of accomplishing anything "we set our minds to." That says it all: if we set our minds to it, we can do it. But if we allow our minds to believe that the possible is impossible, then we are doomed to fail.

Some compare life to a rat race, running around in a maze, trying to escape. I'm not trying to escape life, though. I'm trying to prevail, or as the song from that old Teen Wolf movie (with Michael J. Fox) says, I'm just trying to "win in the end". So for me, life is more like one of those hurdle races. I see the obstacles. I chose to run the race. I leap over those obstacles, after some intense training of course. And then I cross that finish line because I made a conscious decision from the beginning that my sights are set on the finish line, not the hurdles. The hurdles are only a physical challenge. The hurdles are within my vision, but they are not the end result that I envision. Winning in the end is a feat empowered by the mind, by a mentality. And only a mentality can draw you from your course.

Recently, I started jogging again. I run for about 30 minutes, outside, Rocky Balboa style (no monumental race to any top of the stairs, but there's at least two mighty hills to conquer on my run). The first time, I didn't make it all the way. In retrospect, I wasn't out of breath nor was I out of shape. I was a little unfocused. Where was my focus? All I could think about was how I wasn't sure if I could make it all the way. I kept

BEYOND LIMITATIONS

thinking I want this to end soon because I can't take it anymore. I was defeated by my own mind. The very next run was successful. I stayed mentally focused. I was determined to make it all the way. I accepted that I wasn't ready to sprint the entire way and that was fine. After all, it's like I said in one of my speeches, overnight success is a myth; a patient person has a greater chance to succeed as opposed to an impatient person, because a patient person can accept that success takes time. It takes time; it takes development; and it takes the right "mentality".

So do I think I can fly? Do I think I can lift a skyscraper with my bare hands? Of course not. I'm realistic. We need to be in order to achieve our goals. But being realistic doesn't mean that we convince ourselves that we can't do it or that it can't be done. Being realistic just means that we will strategically devise a step-by-step plan to surpass the limits that in actuality do not exist.

This message is dedicated to the 9th and 10th graders I worked with 14 years ago. In a theatrical competition in which they were pitted against two other teams: the juniors and the seniors; no one wasted time considering that they could win. They were too young. They were too inexperienced. They didn't have the developed talent of the upperclassmen to pull off a victory. The young kids only competed because there needed to be three teams, and because they needed to learn how to run the race before they could win the race. They shocked the crowd. They did the unthinkable. They did what had never been done before. I remember speaking to them before they took the stage. My message was clear. "If you want this, then it's yours." It's all about believing in yourself and believing in your abilities. The joy on their faces said it all. They went on to win the competition two more times before they graduated, achieving a record setting three out of four victories. More importantly, they graduated with an early lesson in life:

"What we perceive (or even what others perceive) as our limitations are often only mental obstacles."

BEYOND LIMITATIONS

Quote: "No matter who you are, or what you've achieved in the past, you have to work hard every time in order to win. Lose the fire in your belly and you've opened the door to defeat." - Sam Wyly

They made the decision for me. I was just an innocent bystander caught in the middle of a battle of the sexes. The girls rallied behind the new kid. They said she was the new fastest runner in school. But the boys said that I was the fastest runner in school. After all, I was the fastest kid on the track team. I was the superstar of the team. But I was hesitant to race her. I didn't know why I felt that way, but I just didn't want to do it. But I couldn't let down the boys. So without warming up, without stretching, without a practice run, and without giving myself some time to mentally and physically prepare, I rode the wave of my fans to the playground. And several seconds after taking that runner's stance, I lost the most important unofficial race I ever ran. It didn't even matter that after she officially joined the track team, I beat her in a practice drill. Running track was never the same for me. I was only in the fifth grade. It was an important lesson to learn at such an early age. If only I had approached that race differently, I might have never experienced the abatement of my desire to be a track star. I was a star but the star had faded. It was that early that I learned that "No matter who you are, or what you've achieved in the past, you have to work hard every time in order to win. Lose the fire in your belly and you've opened the door to defeat." - Sam Wyly.

Yes, I tried track and field again in middle school. I even considered running track in college, but the fire was gone. Never lose your steam.

Never allow one defeat to stop you. Instead, learn from that defeat. Work harder after that defeat.

And never lose your drive. When you lose your fire, all you gain is regret. Secondly, believe in yourself, but don't believe the hype. Self-confidence will breed success. Hype will diffuse the hard work one needs to succeed.

Every year, I tell my students that my favorite vocabulary word is

BEYOND LIMITATIONS

"assiduous". Assiduous means hardworking. And then I tell them that the difference between a successful person and a person who is not as successful as he potentially could be is "work ethic". You can have all the knowledge in the world; you can have all the tools, all the skills, and all the ability. But the knowledge and ability to do something is meaningless if it's not put to action. You have to put in the work. And so I tell my students that by the end of the year, one life lesson I want them to learn and adopt is "You have to work hard every time in order to win."

But there's another key part of that lesson that cannot be ignored: "Lose the fire in your belly and you've opened the door to defeat."

Have you ever watched a Rocky movie? Don't they just get you fired up? Well, there's one very memorable scene from Rocky III that I will never forget. It's the scene that ends the first fight Rocky had with Clubber Lang (played by Mr. T). It was quick. It was painful. Rocky's head bounced off the mat in defeat.

And it was no surprise if you paid attention to the beginning of the film. Rocky got caught up in the glitz, the glamour, the fame, the fortune; most importantly, he got caught up in his own success. Distracted by the benefits of his achievements and losing his head in his own press clippings, he stopped training. Apollo Creed said it best later in the film: Rocky had lost the eye of the tiger.

In my speech "Exercising to Be Effective, I concluded with the quote "Excellence is not an accomplishment; it's a never ending process." I learned a long time ago that goal setting is invaluable. But the danger in achieving one's goal is satisfaction and complacency. In life, it's not enough to win the prize. The real goal is to keep it. And the only way to keep it is to keep working as if the excellence you wish to achieve is only another step up that ladder.

Sure, it's okay to celebrate success. You have to celebrate your milestones.

BEYOND LIMITATIONS

Success isn't as sweet without a victory lap or an ice-cold cooler of Gatorade.

But after the party, you must return to work because the achievement of another goal, another victory, another moment of success is the fuel that ignites the fire, the fire we need to achieve success every single time.

So always remember: Without the fire, there is no victory.

Be the fire.

Be the flame.

Be the undefeated.

BEYOND LIMITATIONS

Quote: "If you wallow in your own internal housekeeping – restraining personal demons, comparing yourself to other people, worrying about things you can't change – then you don't have the mental energy left to figure out where you want to go and how to get there." - Sam Wyly

Life is a mental game. That's what it comes down to. It doesn't matter what else is going on; if your mind is out of the game, you will lose. If your mind is not focused, you will lose sight of what you need to do, what you want to accomplish. Sometimes, life is hard. So many good things don't happen to people who feel they deserve something because they have worked so hard.

I may have just missed the biggest opportunity of my life. The New Jersey Nets held an audition to find a new announcer for their Brooklyn Stadium. That's the perfect job for me. When I heard the news, twelve hours too late, I was crushed. I'm still lamenting over it to this day. And all these thoughts keep racing through my head: how is it possible that of all the people I know, no one had heard the word so that they could tell me?

Pause

A good friend of mine did send me a text message 8 hours before the audition...the audition which was held within walking distance (ok, 4 train stops from my house...whatever...it was so close). Other thoughts crashed through my head: If only I had upgraded my phone a month ago when I had the opportunity, I would have received the message. I started to have problems with my phone the Tuesday before the audition. That prevented me from checking my messages on the regular as I always do. The tracking ball on my crackberry broke. I couldn't scroll down one day. I couldn't scroll up the next day. I had to take out the battery and put it back in just so I could see my most recent messages. How annoying. So

BEYOND LIMITATIONS

I didn't see my friend's message until hours after I had asked myself, "How is it that out of all the people I know, no one heard about this?" Seeing the message was like a twist of the knife in a wounded heart.

An opportunity: gone.

Sigh.

Wait...wait...I couldn't give up so easily. There had to be something I could do. I had one contact with the New Jersey Nets. I sent him an email Saturday afternoon.

I just heard news this morning that the Nets had an audition for a new announcer. That's me! I can't believe I heard about this 24 hours too late. But I would like to at least try to seize an opportunity. I'm very interested. I've been called the "Voice of Brooklyn Tech". Now I could be the "Voice of the Brooklyn Nets"! I hoping you can be my gateway and the one to discover the "Voice". If there's someone you can send this link to, then you and everyone else will see how I can ignite a crowd!

Monday morning, he wrote back.

Unfortunately, it was a one-day try out. If for some reason there are additional tryouts, I will let you know.

My heart sunk lower. More thoughts made it worse. Why did the auditions have to happen during a four-day weekend? I'm a teacher. Had I been at work, which is literally walking distance from where the auditions were held, I would have been there. The friend who sent me the text message...she works at my school...I would have gotten the word.

BEYOND LIMITATIONS

Sigh

No...no sigh...no sighing.

In life, many opportunities will pass us by. Sometimes, we will miss those opportunities because of something we could have done.

Being too cheap to get a phone upgrade.

We can't waste time and energy finding blame within ourselves or cursing out our personal demons. Doing so doesn't bring back the opportunity.

Stay focused on your goal.

You can't control when the next opportunity will present itself. And you may even miss that one too. But you'll never be ready to capture any opportunity if you lose your focus.

In life, there will be many missed opportunities. We will miss some, while others seize the moment. Do you know how hard it was to watch the two people who were interviewed on the news about their audition?

Why them?

Why not me?

We can't waste our time and energy worrying about what other people do or have. There are a lot of people chasing the same dreams. Let them have their dreams. The world is big enough for everybody to realize his or her dreams. This may have been a perfect job for me. But I will persist. There's another perfect dream that will match my aspirations.

Our goals are not impeded by others who share those goals.

Our goals are impeded only by what we allow to discourage us.

BEYOND LIMITATIONS

I can't turn back the hands of time. I can't change the fact that there were only auditions for one day. I can't change the fact that I missed an opportunity. So instead of wasting my time and energy on worrying about what happened or didn't happen in the past and what I can't change, I choose to use my time, my mental energy on continuing towards my goal.

All that matters is moving forward, regardless of our flaws, regardless of what others have achieved, regardless of what we can't change.

"If you wallow in your own internal housekeeping – restraining personal demons, comparing yourself to other people, worrying about things you can't change – then you don't have the mental energy left to figure out where you want to go and how to get there." - Sam Wyly

Stay focused.

Empower your mental energy.

And you will succeed.

BEYOND LIMITATIONS

Quote: "You need to protect your good idea from other people's negativity until it's out of it's infancy." - Mary Baker Eddy

This is not to say that the people with whom we keep company are negative. This actually has nothing to do with other people. This has everything to do with you and only you.

Years ago, I told a friend that I wanted to pursue the field of professional speaking. That was a mistake. He's actually a close friend of mine, someone who has an opinion that I deeply respect. But when I ponder why I told him my aspiration, I realized that it was because I was looking for two things: motivation and approval.

I figured if I told someone what my aspirations were then I would be obligated, maybe even pressured to pursue my goals. Notice the word "pressure". Who needs to be pressured to do what you want to do. But that's what "that kind" of motivation does. So, if you say you're going to do it but don't do it, then you'll be the one with the egg on your own face.

And why was there egg on my face? Because I didn't understand, at the time, that the "best type" of motivation is "self-motivation". I can write weekly motivations, monthly motivations, or even hourly motivations that I can only hope will lift your spirits or light a fire under you. But until you find it within yourself to motivate yourself, no one else can get you to do it, no one else can give you that spark. Those closest to us will hopefully be supportive of what motivates us, but true motivation is internal.

It's been about six years since I told my friend about my plan to become a professional speaker….six years because I lost steam…six years, because only until recently did I find the self-motivation. And then, when I decided to pursue my dream (because telling people what I want to do is a hell of a lot different than actually doing something), I started watching workshop videos about public speaking. Only my wife knew. Then I started working on my website. Only my wife knew, until I finished it. I do imagine that some people might have been skeptical.

Soon, these people say things and imply things that are unintentional but dangerous because they cause self-doubt, the antithesis of self-motivation.

BEYOND LIMITATIONS

So sharing your goals with an audience to create a binding contract of sorts is really a way to simply watch your dreams bust away at the seams.

It has been actually much more helpful to share the realization of a short-term goal and utilize the feedback to get me closer to a long-term goal. Only after I put the final touch on my site, did I spread the word. No matter what feedback I got, I was confident because of what I had already accomplished.

Think about it...the inception of any accomplishment is born from a desire to do what YOU want to do. We don't need to tell anyone what we plan to do in order to get it done. We only need to tell others what we have done because feedback at that stage is most valuable as it serves to refine our plans, not define our plans.

No one can define who you are and yet we often act according to the judgment, criticism, or approval of others. As a public speaker, I am intrigued by the thought that the reason why public speaking is feared almost as much as death is because we are afraid to be judged. And yet, as much as we fear judgment, we crave approval. But why? We don't want to be judged because of any insecurities we might possess. We're afraid that someone will discover a flaw, a mistake, a blemish, a shortcoming. Approval, on the other hand, is what we crave because we relish being told how great we think we are. Who doesn't love a compliment? But I'd rather allow someone the opportunity to compliment what I have achieved, then allow someone to criticize, second-guess, or redirect what I'd like to achieve. Besides, the greatest compliment is the one you give to yourself.

It all comes back to self-motivation, self-confidence, self-assurance: "self". I can be a very humble guy, but in my mind, I believe great things about myself. And so, when I finally decided to pursue my goal, it was not because I wanted someone to be proud of what I am trying to do and it wasn't because I needed someone to take notice. My pursuit is simply about me: what I am capable of doing, what I have done thus far, what I will do, and how happy I will be with what I've done.

BEYOND LIMITATIONS

But here's the key, I chose this path and I paved the road. And only after I paved the first road, did I open it up for others to see.

If there's something you want to do,

Devise your plan privately,

Identify your steps independently

Accomplish you initial goal exclusively.

"You need to protect your good idea from other people's negativity until it's out of it's infancy." - Mary Baker Eddy

And then once you have achieved self-actualization, you will experience self-confidence, and arrive at the realization that once you have already laid down the foundation for your success, everyone else is just there for the ride.

Success is a locomotive steered by a single visionary who sees the light at the end of a tunnel. The conductor who welcomes the backseat drivers into his engine room, is blinded by the flashing lights, falls off the track, and never makes it out of the tunnel.

Share your vision only after you shed some light.

And remember that success is an invention concocted in a laboratory, not on a stage.

BEYOND LIMITATIONS

A Proud Man's Journey

Quote: "There are no failures in a journey to success. There are only opportunities to learn how to succeed on the next level."

The 2011 Toastmasters International District 46 Humorous Speech Contest has come to an end. And though I was not named THE winner, I am a WINNER. Only eight months after joining the international club, I participated in my first contest and advanced to the final round competing against the best of the best.

Yes, I am disappointed, but that's the way it should be; my disappointment is a testament to my passion. You can't achieve success without passion. And you can't build character without disappointment. So often, people get discouraged when they don't get what they want. Those who are discouraged fail. Those who are disappointed are motivated to make the most of the next opportunity. There will always be other opportunities. That's why we must simply reflect on our performance, tweak it and enhance it, and then seize the next opportunity.

And we must always remember that the hardest thing to accept about success, is that it takes time; it's a journey.

And I gained a lot from my most recent trip on this journey.

In August 2010, I heard about an opportunity to be a target speaker for another local Brooklyn Toastmasters club. I signed up right away so that I could speak in front of and network with a new group of people. I am beginning to build my ability to network. Penny Loretto wrote, "Over the course of your lifetime, networking will be the single most effective strategy used in advancing your career. Learning the skills for effective networking is worth the time and energy it requires since it's such an important aspect [of your pursuit to succeed]." I didn't get to deliver the speech though. They double booked target speakers. So I was out and left with "For Love, We are Fools".

At the following LIU Toastmasters Club meeting in September, an announcement was made about the 2011 Humorous Speech Contest. I wasn't too sure about this one. After all, humor is not my comfort zone.

BEYOND LIMITATIONS

I can deliver a speech to persuade or to inform with doses of humor, but delivering a speech with the primary intent to make people laugh....let's just say, that's like Michael Jordan taking a break from basketball to play baseball. And we all know how that turned out. But we all know how that turned out because he tried. He stepped out of his comfort zone. And I did too.

Strength and Character are built on new adventures and unchartered territories. There is no reward without risk.

No one else signed up to compete in the club competition, so I automatically advanced to the next round. That was lucky. But the best part was not the advance, but the advice.

I had the chance to practice in front of my fellow members and here's what I learned:

- Dialogue is the spice of any good story. Nothing brings your story to life better than what people actually said. Although, embellishing the dialogue works too.

- Slow down your pace. Give your audience a chance to enjoy your speech. Your speech isn't like a movie that they can watch again or rewind to their favorite part. The pause serves no better purpose when you're waiting for your audience to finish laughing.

- Be careful when you use video. Using visual aids is encouraged, but you don't always need a video to tell the story. YOU can do it. I had this video clip all set up (from an episode of the Cosby Show). At the Area competition, when I pressed start, nothing happened. I had to adjust quickly. Minutes later, in the middle of the speech, the video started playing. I had to adjust again. Then, upon entering the room for the Division contest, I didn't see a video screen set up. What would I do? I replayed the video clip in my head and composed my narration of the scene. Never let the panic throw you off your game. Never let them see you sweat.

BEYOND LIMITATIONS

* The key to not allowing anything to distract you, including unplanned occurrences: Preparation. As I always like to say, "Your Performance is only as good as your Preparation. Because I practiced, practiced, practiced, my speech was internalized. I advanced to the Division contest. That was the last time I used the video.

On the night of the Division Contest, I drew #6 and watched some excellent speeches. And all I could remember were the words of another fellow Toastmaster who said, "Just have fun." She's right. Why else do we do what we love? No matter what happened, I had to enjoy myself up there. We will never experience true success if we don't experience any joy from the success we pursue and achieve.

And then came the District Contest. I made it to the finals. The best of the best would take the stage. There were former competitors who had advanced to the finals before. There were long-term Toastmasters who would be named DTMs that very night. What a great experience! I walked on the stage to get a feel for the room when the contest chair advised me to think of how I could incorporate the words of the keynote speaker. *"Listen, it's okay to have drive like Dana Lamon. It's just not okay to drive like Dana Lamon."* For those who don't know, the keynote speaker and 1992 World Champion of Public Speaking is blind.

The lesson is to always be able to think on your feet. Preparation is key; this is true. But spontaneity is the advantage.

There are many lessons to be learned along the way. First place: he delivered the most universal message about telling little white lies. Second place: his use of props was very emphatic as he threw to the floor every meaningless gift you could give to your spouse. Third place: her dramatization visually told the story, especially when she imitated the gossiping women in church. The greatest value of my experience was the observations I made and the lessons I learned. I didn't win. I didn't even place in the top three. But I reflected. I learned.

And most importantly, I remain focused, motivated, and encouraged.

BEYOND LIMITATIONS

"Success is a matter of understanding and religiously practicing specific, simple habits that always lead to success." - Robert J. Ringer

You ever think to yourself, "I have way too many things to do, and there are just not enough hours in the day"? I find myself thinking that all the time. Sometimes, I wonder if it's possible to get it all done by whatever deadlines I have. But I know it's possible because it all gets done eventually. I just always remind myself of the title of that book, Don't Sweat the Small Stuff.

That's great advice, but that only addresses one particular issue for me. It stops the panic and the anxiety. I stress a lot less when I tell myself, don't lose the cool; I'll get it done. And it gets done because at the twelfth hour when I have no choice but to get it done, I focus, I eliminate all distractions, and I go to task. Unfortunately, that's usually 30 minutes before a meeting, 15 minutes before I have to leave the house, or during the late hours when I'm fighting to keep my eyes open while shoving snacks down my mouth to stay awake. That can't possibly be an effective plan, but it's often the plan many of us use.

Having the mentality that the work will get done helps, but that doesn't address how to get it done. As I often like to say, there is no success without the combination of motivation and strategies. And by strategies, I mean those "specific, simple habits". And my life changed once I discovered a habit I like to call "30 Minutes of Productivity". And now I recommend it to everyone.

So one day a student came to me to ask about advice for a literature essay she had to write. She had to compare two books, but didn't have a second book to fit the quote of the assignment. I suggested a book. She had not read it. I suggested another book. She had not read that one either.

Wait...wait...wait. I tried a different approach. What books had she read? Whatever she read didn't fit the quote. So I suggested one more book, a short one...because she "snuck in" a very important detail that she should have told me when she first walked into my office: that her deadline was in two days.

BEYOND LIMITATIONS

Anybody see the problem here?

Why did she wait until the last minute? When was the essay assigned? Two weeks before the week-long break? Really? When she came to me, it was two days after we had returned from the break.

Of course I asked her. And of course she gave that look that most students give...you know, the look that says, "I know I shouldn't wait 'til the last minute."

But then she said what I always hear: "But I work better under pressure. I do my best work and get my best grades when I wait until the last minute."

And yes, she is right and yet, she is so wrong.

Attention all procrastinators...sorry, name-calling won't get me anywhere. Attention all beat the clock, greatest success at the last minute experts: It's not that you produce your best work because you work great under pressure. Rather, you produce your best work because you work great when you are focused.

Think about it: at that proverbial twelfth hour, at the proverbial last minute, you have no other choice but to eliminate all distractions, buckle down, and zero in on your work. You have no other choice because you have given yourself no other choice. But that's only because you haven't considered that your best work is not a product of time, or pressure, but rather a product of focus.

One profound message I remember from my college orientation was that the best, most successful students tend to be student-athletes. Because of their packed schedules, these athletes have no other choice but to focus because they don't have the time to waste.

So here's my suggestion: I call it 60 Minutes of Productivity (though for students, 30 minutes might be more practical considering all the classes they take).

Step 1: Identify/List the tasks you need to complete.

Step 2: Consider the order in which those tasks should be done (consider placing near the top those tasks that you find most difficult and those that require a high level of concentration).

Step 3: Set your clock for 60 minutes and go to task.

Now, how funny is it that I'm suggesting a strategy that is driven by a time limit. Doesn't that contradict my whole point?

Ok, listen carefully: it's not the pressure of time that is the effective means of being productive; rather, it's the management of time, or rather the management of focus.

My strategy is actually the best of both worlds because it's obviously true that you work well against the clock, but only because you are focused.

I could see the apprehension in her eyes. If you can focus under pressure at the last minute, then why focus any earlier? You must be thinking, "I can spend my time doing other things first if my last minute focus will get me the same results as time-managed focus."

Hey, I like that term: time-managed focus...I just made that up.

Back to your question: Now that's just silly. Anything you work on at the last minute might very well be great work...but your best? No work is better than the work you do in advance because the advantage of work in advance is the opportunity to review, reflect, and revise. The disadvantage to down-to-the-last-minute work is that "it is what it is; good or bad; there's nothing you can do about it now." That's not your best work. That's just completed work...maybe. If you're working under the guise of you work well under pressure, then it's time to adopt a new habit. What may work occasionally is not a productive plan. It's just a stroke of luck. And luck is not a strategy for success.

I have been experimenting with my 60 Minutes of Productivity since the new-year began. I'm getting more things done. I'm able to work on multiple projects over the course of a long period of time. I am able to work on tasks without feeling rushed or stressed. I'm able to do my tasks without feeling consumed by one task; so the task does not feel like a drag or a burden. And I'm able to take a much needed break, during the day, to re-energize and refocus; working through breaks is becoming a thing of the past. Why? Three reasons: I have focus, I have a strategy, and I have seen the results.

BEYOND LIMITATIONS

I've shared this strategy with the students in my classes. The first time I recommended 30 Minutes of Productivity to my students, I asked them to let me know if it worked for them. Two days later, this is what they shared.

One student said that she actually tried 60 minutes. She logged on to Facebook and told her friends that she would be off-line for one hour so that she could do her work. She focused on her assignment and completed the task with ease. The strategy worked for her.

Another student A.K wrote, "Yesterday I set aside about an hour to do work. I just sat down and did nothing but work, without letting anything distract me. After an hour, I had finished. Instead of staying up till 12 o'clock, I went to bed at 9:30, which was 8 hours of sleep for me because I woke up at 5:30. I felt much more rested and focused."

N.M. wrote, "When I tried the 30 minute no distraction method; it didn't work for me. I sat down to do my work, but it was so quiet that I couldn't concentrate. In order for me to finish I had to put on some music. I suppose that without the Facebook page and email open, my homework took less time than before, but as far as no distractions, that doesn't work for me."

And D.Z. added, "On January 13, 2012, I set 90 minutes to study for my Social Studies Exam about Rome. Rome was a huge topic to talk about and I had a lot of notes on it. I shut off my laptop to prevent distractions. I can get really distracted by people aiming me on Aim. I even closed my door and put a post-it on the door that read, " Do not bother me! Studying for a test!" I didn't want my family coming into my room bothering me. I had 25 pages of notes front and back to review and memorize. I couldn't waste time. Therefore, I started reviewing the notes. Instead of spending 90 minutes studying, I spent 60 minutes reviewing my notes. I had the other 30 minutes to study for my Spelling Quiz and Vocabulary Quiz. Like Mr. Williams said, 'If you set your mind to do something, you can do it.'"

Like Mr. Williams said," If you set your mind to do something, you can do it." I say that because I believe it. But if there's one valuable lesson I've learned over the past few months; it's that just as much as we need motivation, we also need strategies.

So whenever we feel like we have too many things to do and not enough hours in the day, I recommend we take control of that time by setting our stopwatches to 30 or 60 minutes. Then we should work non-stop for the duration of the time without any interruptions. Uninterrupted productivity is the best kind that there is. And seeing the end in sight as opposed to thinking of every task as an endless chore can push us. And even if we cannot finish that task within that 30 or 60 minute time limit, that's okay. We can take a break and then come back to it. Studies show that we're actually much more effective when we take breaks at 30 or 60 minute intervals. We relieve ourselves of stress, anxiety, and tiredness. And our retention of information actually increases when we work in intervals.

My students confirmed that it can be 30 minutes or 60 minutes (by the way, notice that the student who worked for 90 minutes actually worked for 60 minutes on history and 30 minutes on English) but the amount of time, whether it is 30, 60, or somewhere in between, does not matter. It can be "X"" Minutes of Productivity. What matters are the focus and a strategy that can become a routine. So set whatever time limit works for you towards your Productivity; just make sure you follow a plan and develop a routine to be productive.

"The individual who wants to reach the top in business must appreciate the might and force of habit. He must be quick to break those habits that can break him—and hasten to adopt those practices that will become the habits that help him achieve the success he desires."
-J. Paul Getty

BEYOND LIMITATIONS

Quote: "You have to prepare to be the best because your performance is only as great as your preparation."

Can anyone truly claim to be the best in the world at what they do?

That's quite the title to claim. Sure, there are many who can lay the claim: the Muhammad Ali's and Mike Tyson's, the Michael Jordan's and Kobe Bryant's, the Dan Marino's and Joe Montana's, and the late and greats like James Brown or Michael Jackson. But if there are so many great ones, so many who can claim to be the best, then doesn't that mean that being the best isn't the real focus. We can all be the best, but we can't achieve a spot among the best if we don't do what the best in the world do best.

Practice

Michael Buffer made the words famous, "Are you ready?" But he didn't simply mean, "are you ready to be called the best?" No, no, no, because that's a rhetorical question. Of course, we all are ready to be "called" the best. But there is no effort in being "called" the best. There is no glory in that that. That's just a pipe dream. You have to put in a lot of work to make that a reality.

So what he meant was, "Are you ready?" Did you put in the practice necessary to step up to all the challenges along the way?

"Are you ready?" Did you prepare every aspect of your game to maximize your potential and excel above and beyond your peak?

The truth is if you aim to be the best, then you can achieve your goal...Good.

But aiming will never be good enough.

So you have to ask yourself this question, "Do you want to be the best at what you do, or do you only want to be good enough to get the job done? Personally, I want to be the best I can be.

Currently, I'm on a journey to become the World Champion of Public Speaking…the best in the world at what I do.

And the hardest part about this journey is that the end result, at any level, lies in the judgment, the opinion of others. But that's okay, because the end result is secondary to the process….to the practice.

It's secondary because without the process, there is no end result. The process is the missing link that many people don't really get.

You have to practice.

You have to prepare.

Don't you know the story? Michael Jordan sucked as a basketball player when he was a kid. Do you know how much practice he must have put in to be the best in the world at what he did?

Regardless of how you feel about rapper Lil' Wayne, after watching so many documentaries about him, I learned that he eats, bleeds, and sleeps his craft. And from what I understand, the "sleep" is not really much of the equation.

You have to practice.

You have to prepare.

In 1996, I was the advisor for a group of 9th and 10th graders who were competing in a competition called SING. Three weeks before the show, the 11th graders and 12th graders were still putting the pieces of their show together. Meanwhile, I had those 9th and 10th graders running full rehearsals: costumes, props, set changes, no scripts. On the day of the

BEYOND LIMITATIONS

official school-wide dress rehearsal, the music director looked at me and said, "They're gonna win!" And he was right! They did!

But he didn't know that because he had some kind of second sight.

Rather, he knew that because he could see....

He could see that they were prepared.

You have to practice.

You have to prepare.

As I prepare for the third round of competition, I realize that it's true, I could probably write a book about public speaking, but I still read articles written by those who have prepared to be the best. I do that so that I can continue to learn…continue to prepare.

I could probably take the stage now if today were the day of the next round. But in the meantime, I'm watching former World Champions on YouTube. The other night, I was watching on the Science Channel an episode of TedTalks Science. My wife turned around and said, "What are you watching?" The speaker Bonnie Bassler was talking about how cells communicate with each other. My wife said, "You can't possibly be interested in this." But she didn't understand. It was not the subject matter that interests me. It was the delivery of the presentation that was of interest to me.

Just like other professionals, I study tapes. And then I stand up in my living room, late at night and practice my speech.

You have to practice.

You have to prepare.

It's like that old saying, "Practice makes perfect." Or rather it's like my new saying, "You must prepare to be the best because your performance is only as great as your preparation."

So Practice, Practice, Practice.

BEYOND LIMITATIONS

Practice every chance you get.

Every day when I walk home, I practice a speech.

Practice like it's the real thing.

Remember, a rehearsal is nothing but a show in advance.

Practice, not only what you plan to perform.

Practice to perfect what you will perform.

Prepare, Prepare, Prepare.

"It's not the will to win that matters—everyone has that. It's the will to prepare to win that matters." -Paul "Bear" Bryant

Now, if you don't mind I have to go practice.

BEYOND LIMITATIONS

Put a little P.E.P. in Your Step

I want you to remember three letters: P.E.P: Positivity Exudes Productivity. If you want to be more productive, then you have to have a positive approach to everything you do. And so tonight, I want to take this P.E.P. mentality and teach you that one of the best ways to achieve and maintain success is by taking care of yourself and living a positive lifestyle. In other words, I want to teach you how to put a little P.E.P. in your S.T.E.P. Come on everybody; stand up and do this step with me. S.T.E.P.: Secure your Success by Taking a Break, Eating Right, and Pumping It Up. Ok everybody: Stop, take a seat, and think about this.

According to the on-line health magazine, Journey to Wellness, we have a limited amount of energy. On a daily basis, we put a lot of wear and tear on our bodies. Luckily, our bodies are designed to repair themselves and restore that energy. So what do we do? We push our bodies beyond the limit; we keep going and going and going; we keep depriving our bodies of the sleep and rest we need. And as a result, we don't leave our bodies with enough energy to heal, and as a result, we feel fatigued and sick. Furthermore, it's a scientific fact that when we don't get enough sleep and rest, we get grumpy, less patient, and short-tempered. In other words, we get negative. And let's be honest, even when we're not running around trying to do everything, we're still thinking so much that all that mental chatter just causes mental strain, and that is not rest. Trust me; I know because about three months ago, for the first time since I was born, I was admitted to the hospital. For twelve straight hours, I was struggling to breathe; I was gasping for air. And despite all the tests the doctors gave me, they couldn't figure out what was wrong. They had no answers. Then my aunt walked into the hospital and said, "I think you've got a lot of stress; you're working extremely hard; and you're not taking care of yourself. And she was right. And it's funny that she said that because the best test I took was a pulmonary function test (a breathing test). The technician told me, "For the next few minutes, breathe deeply into this tube." Come on everybody; do it with me. I don't know if it was three, five, or ten minutes; all I know is that when he said, "'You can stop," I opened my eyes and said, "Wow! I've got to do that more often. I can't remember the last time I felt that relaxed." So, I implore you: daily, for at least three minutes, close your eyes, clear your mind, and breathe deeply, because according to the Textbook of Natural Medicine, all the things that happen to our bodies when we are stressed (when we're feeling negative): the increased heart rate, the fast breathing, the high blood pressure, all decrease when we breathe deeply to relax. Now that's positive.

Now, when I was in the hospital, I ate hospital food, which wasn't as bad as I had expected. And it got me to start thinking about my diet. And when I did a little research, I was not surprised by what I found. Like most people, I snack too much. As a matter of fact, according to the International Deli-Dairy- Bakery Association, 90% of us snack throughout the day, which is more than the amount of people who eat lunch and the amount of people who eat breakfast. And statistics show that snacking is becoming more acceptable. And that's bad because we're moving away from snacking between meals to snacking in place of meals. And nutrition experts say that's bad because as we snack in place of meals, we lose track of how much we're eating and we damage our bodies. It is recommended that we limit ourselves to two healthy snacks a day. I suggest pistachio nuts because they lower our cholesterol and improve the health of our hearts, and dark chocolate because it is scientifically proven to lower our blood pressure and improve our blood flow. Remember, experts say that two healthy snacks and three meals per day will give us the energy we need to be productive.

Finally, my favorite test was the stress test. They put you on a treadmill, increase the speed, and increase the incline. It is great exercise for someone who doesn't exercise like he should. And why don't I exercise like I should? Well according to "Stuck on the Couch" by Sanjay Gupta, "A lot of people don't like to exercise, so it's the first thing to go when we have an opportunity to rearrange our schedule." And even though we know we should exercise, after a long day, many of us don't have the self-discipline to stick to a fitness routine. But I say forget waiting until the end of the day and instead, do some daily moderate exercise during the day. We all walk. Just walk quicker. That's moderate exercise. But let me share with you another moderate exercise: pyramid jumping jacks. You do jumping jacks for ten seconds; rest for ten seconds; jumping jacks for twenty seconds; rest for twenty seconds;

jumping jacks for thirty seconds; rest for thirty seconds. Then do the same thing in reverse order. It takes just about four minutes. And you can do it anywhere, any time, a few times a day. Remember, fitness expert Wayne McGregor said that daily moderate exercise can dramatically improve our health and help us fight depression, anxiety, and stress. And, it can leave us with a sharper mind, more energy, and a positive outlook. And at the end of the day, that's what it's all about, because Positivity Exudes Productivity.

So can we all put a little P.E.P. in our S.T.E.P.? Of course we can. Can we take care of ourselves and live a positive lifestyle so that we can achieve and maintain success? Of course we can. Because with a positive attitude, we can do anything we want. So I will leave you with the words I wrote in an email the day I left the hospital: With a positive mind, an energetic spirit, and a capable body, we must always find time to take care of ourselves. Because when we take care of ourselves, we are able to climb higher mountains and accomplish so much more than we are already able to achieve.

BEYOND LIMITATIONS

Quote: "Excellence is a better teacher than mediocrity. The lessons of the ordinary are everywhere. Truly profound and original insights are to be found only in studying the exemplary."
-Warren G. Bennis

After all my research, what I have found is that most of the experts on effective study habits express a lot of the same thoughts and offer the same tips. And yet, we still have a number of children who are either not successful students or who are not as successful as they could be. That's because we can be pushed, motivated, and forced to do something, but it never really gets done unless we are self-motivated and self-disciplined to do the things that we know we should do, but don't necessarily want to do.

I think the most important thing we need to remember about self-discipline and self-motivation is that it's no easy task. We may not perfectly nor routinely follow the habits that will make us successful, but we must always work towards consistency.

We must always serve as our own internal cheerleaders.

We must always surround ourselves with motivated peers and role models.

And we must always pursue excellence even though we may never achieve perfection.

We must share our successes, failures, and challenges with someone we trust.

And we must always search for concrete strategies that can help us achieve our goals.

Most importantly, don't allow self-defeat nor frustration with struggle to consume your self-motivation. You can do this. **Keep a positive attitude: There is nothing more powerful for self-motivation than the right attitude. You can't choose or control your circumstance, but can choose your attitude towards your circumstances.**

BEYOND LIMITATIONS

Quote: "The greater danger for most of us lies not in setting our aim too high and falling short; but in setting our aim too low, and achieving our mark." —Michelangelo

From the book "9 1/2 Unbreakable Rules of Marketing", written by my good friend and mentor Cathey Armillas, (page 28), (Consistency Beats Ability): We human beings tend to stick with the familiar; it makes us comfortable." And I'd like to add, that the comfort of one's own mind is a stifling place to be. Comfort can hold us back. When we are satisfied with what we do or even the level at which we do it, we lose grip of the inspiration we need to go further.

"The greater danger for most of us lies not in setting our aim too high and falling short; but in setting our aim too low, and achieving our mark." - Michelangelo

I got an email several months ago about this new development of homes on the beachfront. I took my family to see these homes. They were beautiful. Not growing up in a house, this was my first sight of what my dream house could be. But then I sat down to discuss financing and realized that this dream was way out of my league. I can't afford that. What a tease!

Then I thought, "I'm living very well already. And I should be happy with how far I've come." (How often did I sing the line of that Notorious B.I.G. song "Juicy": "Celebratin' every day, no more public housin'".

I went from the projects, to the very trendy, but very small, but again very trendy apartment in the West Village in NYC, to a bigger place in Queens, to a "deluxe apartment in the sky" (in Jersey), and finally to the upscale Park Slope in Brooklyn.

Yes, I've come a long way, but that word "finally" is troubling. The word

BEYOND LIMITATIONS

finally should never exist in the minds of those who wish to go beyond success. Not that there's anything wrong with celebrating an achievement once you've reached that plateau, but the peak should be somewhere far beyond the clouds.

There are a lot of people who never reach beyond those clouds, not because they're not motivated, but because they only aspire to get off the ground. But while one's vertical leap could be record setting, it will never compare to leaping out of a plane to skydive.

There are also a lot of people who never reach beyond those clouds, not because they're not motivated, but because they are satisfied. And satisfaction doesn't always mean that you've settled for less. For all intents and purposes, you may very well be extremely happy with what you have done in life thus far. And you should be happy and proud.

But don't we all dream about having more; don't we all dream about being more.

I was listening to the radio the other day when I heard the "major" announcement that rapper Lil' Wayne's clothing line Trukfit is expanding beyond skater shops and onto the racks at MACY'S.

Now that's a great example of what one can achieve not only when one aims low and meets the mark, but also when one aims higher.

Now here's a man who has been in the limelight, making money since the age of 11, making enough money to withdraw him from poverty and deposit him into a net worth of 85 million dollars.

He probably doesn't need to work for the rest of his life to live comfortably. He's the hottest thing in pop culture today. So why not stop there?

BEYOND LIMITATIONS

He won't stop because as he says, "He's not a human being." Now for those wondering, what the heck does that mean, for me it's simple.

We have to want to be more than we are defined to be.

Shakespeare said what a piece of a work is a man, implying that we are the pinnacle of beings. But in life, we can go way beyond the pinnacle because we can redefine success every single time. And even if we fail to redefine that success, or fail to achieve more, that's okay, because simply attempting to rise above the occasion is better than coasting.

We can always achieve more. But we must aim to do it. And we must not be afraid to fail or be discouraged by failure. One cannot succeed without failure. And one cannot fail without an attempt. Some of the greatest success stories in the history of the world were written, not necessarily by those who have achieved, but rather by those who dared to do what they, and even others, thought could never be done.

Aim High. Then Aim Beyond.

Lil' Wayne may be ultra-confident in his abilities, but more importantly, he's probably just as ultra-comfortable with failure. You have to be if you want to achieve beyond. So he just won't stop. And you know what probably keeps him going? It's surely the knowledge that with every attempt to excel, there is failure.

And that failure builds the character, knowledge, and skills to help us succeed the next time we attempt to aim beyond.

"The greater danger for most of us lies not in setting our aim too high and falling short; but in setting our aim too low, and achieving our mark." - Michelangelo

In other words, we are all greater than we have proven ourselves to be.

BEYOND LIMITATIONS

And in some cases, we are all greater than we have accepted ourselves to be. So we need to just go for what we want and not just fall back on what we have.

Now granted, Lil' Wayne probably feels a little more comfortable pursuing ventures beyond his success because he has achieved so much. After all, there seemingly is no great risk soaring beyond the clouds when you're already flying with the birds (pun intended by the way), but remember, for him it all began with a bold approach. The nerve he had, as a nine-year old kid, to approach Brian Williams, who was apparently larger than life itself in the world where Wayne grew up, is admirable. He aimed beyond and he rose beyond the occasion.

But not all attempts to rise above are met with success. But had he just accepted being the best rapper on his block, then the block never would have been hot (check his catalog of songs if you don't get that reference).

So I implore you to think about what it is that you have accomplished thus far. And after you pat yourself on the back, as you should, pick up a pen and write down what you would like to accomplish beyond that, something that currently seems out of reach. And if you fall from the sky because you soared so high, remember that with each flight, you grow stronger and you will be able to fly higher each time you try again.

You can never fly if you never try.

And you can never reach the stars if you only try to touch the sky. Don't be afraid to fall. Be afraid to just fly.

Success may be defined by what you achieve, but your definition is written by your aspirations.

118

BEYOND LIMITATIONS

So here's what I want us all to do today: just like the kids who apply to college who are encouraged to pick a safety school and a dream school, let's pick up the pen (it's not official unless it's in writing), write down a safety goal (I want to move to a larger place in Brooklyn that can be an affordable home for my family, where we can live comfortably for the next several years) and then write down the dream goal (the modern beachfront two-story, customized house with the driveway, deck, and backyard). And now we have to investigate the steps to get it done. Tomorrow, let's identify step one.

I wonder if the Wright Brothers wrote such a list. Regardless, consider this: we're able to fly, not only because they weren't afraid to aim beyond (or fly for that matter), but also because they weren't satisfied with just driving to their destination.

Yes, we need drive to get to where we want to be, but with flight, we can go so much further.

And remember, it's better to fly and fall than to just stand tall.

"The greater danger for most of us lies not in setting our aim too high and falling short; but in setting our aim too low, and achieving our mark." - Michelangelo

Why aim to keep your head above water when there are stars to touch beyond the sky?

Today, let's take the vow. Nothing less. Everything more.

BEYOND LIMITATIONS

Quote: "People are about as happy as they make their minds up to be." – Abraham Lincoln

So I was in my living room the other day, watching an old episode of The Flintstones. It was actually the end of the episode but that was all I needed to see because it replayed in my mind the song that I remembered ever since I first heard it, who knows how many years ago.

It's a song that I'm reminded of anytime someone asks me why I'm always so positive. I've always believed that positivity is a choice.

No matter what happened today or didn't happen today; no matter what I failed to do or what I struggled to do; no matter who've I encountered, I never let anything overcome my positive spirit. And to keep that positive spirit, I read positive words, write positive words, or listen to positive words, like the lyrics in the song sung by little Pebbles Flinstone and her little friend Bamm Bamm.

The writers from www.paperchainnetwork.net shared this:

Researchers found that people who typically "forecast" positive outcomes, i.e. they expect things to turn out well are generally happier than those who forecast negative outcomes. They also discovered that people who are deeply engaged with life, both professionally and privately, and who believe their life has a purpose are much happier than those who don't. Researcher Barbara Fredrickson found that optimists reap physical as well as psychological benefits. She has identified the "undo effect" which describes how maintaining a positive mental attitude counters the destructive effects of stress.

George Bernard Shaw once said, "Better keep yourself clean and bright: you are the window through which you must see the world." Positive people, looking through their "clean and bright" windows, simply see

BEYOND LIMITATIONS

many opportunities pessimists miss. Psychologists have named this the "Broaden and Build Theory" and have found that "Positive emotions broaden one's awareness and encourage novel, varied and exploratory thoughts and actions." Simply stated, positive people see and create opportunities that less positive people miss.

Abraham Lincoln was fond of saying "People are about as happy as they make their minds up to be." A positive mental attitude, like anything else of great value, requires regular care and maintenance. Here are a few things to keep your attitude upbeat and positive:

- Make a point of recharging your batteries every day. Read something you find inspirational, listen to motivational CD's or music, or post positive quotations in your workspace etc.
- Watch your words. The words that pass your lips have a profound effect on how you see the world. This will also have a powerful and positive impact on how other people see you.
- Stay away from negative influences. Listen to just enough news to keep yourself informed, and stay away from negative people. If a coworker likes to hold a daily "pity party" tell them "I'd love to talk but I'm quite busy." Take Mark Twain's advice "Keep away from people who belittle your ambitions. Small people always do that, but the really great make you feel that you, too, can become great."
- Keep learning; research shows that the more knowledgeable you are about your job, the more confident you will become. Confidence is an important component of happiness.
- Try to see the bright side of every situation. Think about the two salesmen a shoe company sent to a remote island. The first cabled back, "I quit, no one here wears shoes!" but his replacement sent this message, "Ship supply of shoes immediately-urgent need-no one here has shoes."
- Count your blessings every day, thinking about what is right in your life, instead of dwelling on problems, will make life more enjoyable.
- Take time to relax. Give your brain a rest, find something you enjoy doing and make time for it in your life. It is especially important to spend time with the people who are important in your life.

BEYOND LIMITATIONS

- Have a laugh; few things can lift you up like a hearty laugh. Read a good joke, watch a good comedy and learn to laugh at yourself (Never at others).

In his memoirs, Winston Churchill said, "I am an optimist, it does not seem too much use in being anything else." (www.paperchainnetwork.net)

And as I always like to say, "Misery is a wasted emotion. We should lock it up and throw away the key." A frown will keep you down, but a smile will give you the rise you need.

Remember what I said in my "Words to Be Remembered By" speech:

Be positive! Because I believe that with a positive mind, we can do anything we want. In a recent speech, I said Positivity Exudes Productivity. I love the quote by Brian Tracy, "Keep a positive attitude. There's nothing more powerful for self-motivation, then the right attitude. You can't choose or control your circumstances, but you can choose your attitude towards those circumstances." I say that the circumstances are everything we have to do. The attitude is what gets us through it. So Be Positive.

So Have a Safe, Pleasant, and, POSITIVE Day!

And on that note, I conclude with the words of Pebbles Flintstone and Bamm Bamm Rubble:

"…So let the sun shine in

face it with a grin.

Smilers never lose

and frowners never win…

Open up your heart and let the sun shine in…"

BEYOND LIMITATIONS

Words To Be Remembered By

"Scientific research shows that the power of words can have an effect on our emotions and actions." - Dr. Susan Smiley

Good evening Toastmasters and guests.
As I stand before you, a room full of public speakers, I wonder...do you know the words? There is a bunch of notable people in the world of media who have become famous because of the signature lines they have used to close their shows. For example, Ryan Seacrest ends every episode of American Idol with "Seacrest Out!" I wonder; if I recited a few signature sign-offs, would you be able to tell me who made these words famous?

But what I really want to know is...what words we will be remembered by; why those words; and why do we want to be remembered?

The road to my signature line began shortly after 9/11 when my principal announced that all schools were being encouraged to read the Pledge of Allegiance every morning. I was eventually picked to read the Pledge. Then the Pledge morphed into more announcements: "Attention students, please be reminded that you must submit your lunch applications. Tickets for the School Dance go on sale tomorrow. The Girls Basketball Team is going to the Championships! Go Team!!" The following September, I thought: I have a way to begin the announcements: "Good morning! This is Mr. Williams. I would like to ask everyone to please rise for the Pledge of Allegiance." I have the announcements. Now, I need a way to close the announcements. So I thought about it. What words could I use? Then it came to me..."Have a Safe, Pleasant, and Positive Day!" I like it. "And those have been our announcements for the day; Have a safe, pleasant, and positive day!": Simple. And yet I had no idea that these words would snowball into the fabric and culture of the school. Suddenly, in the hall, a student would say, "Mr. Williams, can you say it 'Have a safe, pleasant, and positive day!'" At graduation, a student would say, "Mr. Williams, can you sign my yearbook, "Have a safe, pleasant, and positive day!'" In my office, a

BEYOND LIMITATIONS

student said, "Mr. Williams, for my economics class, I want to sell a t-shirt with your face on it and the words, 'Have a safe, pleasant, and positive day!'" That's flattering. But even more flattering was the student who said, "Those words are so meaningful to me because they put me in the right frame of mind every morning." It's amazing to have that kind of impact. And that's the power of words. I recently read an article by Dr. Susan Smiley who said that scientific research shows that the power of words can have an effect on our emotions and actions. The words "loving kindness" have been proven to show an increase in self-compassion, an improvement in mood, and a reduction in stress and anxiety. Dr. Martin Luther King Jr. said, "I have a Dream!" Those words will forever transcend and inspire generations. What will our words be? And why those words?

I started to think about that. Of all the words, why did I choose safe, pleasant, and positive? Safe: because we know better and yet we do things we know we shouldn't do. My wife nearly killed a man the other day. It wasn't her fault. The light was green, so he did not have the right of way, but he crossed the street anyway, while looking at his text messages. The other day, a student stopped the elevator by putting his arms between the doors. I said, "How short are our memories." A woman died a few months prior in a tragic NYC elevator accident after she did the same thing. We can only achieve and enjoy success if we live to do it. Be Safe.

Why pleasant? Because as John Maxwell said, "Attitude is Contagious." Have you ever been around someone who's in a bad mood? It's the worse. And the worst part is that a bad mood will drop you faster than a good mood will pick you up. But even though a bad mood works faster, a good mood is more powerful. So smile everybody and spread the joy. People often laugh because when I enter a room sometimes, I scream out, "Hey!" Happy People Make Happy Surroundings. And in Happy Surroundings, we do things that Make Us Happy. So Be Pleasant.

And positive? Because I believe that with a positive mind, we can do anything we want. In a recent speech, I said Positivity Exudes Productivity. I love the quote, "Keep a positive attitude. There's nothing more powerful for self-motivation, then the right attitude. You can't choose or control your circumstances, but you can choose your attitude towards those circumstances." I say that the circumstances are everything we have to do. The attitude is what gets us through it. So Be Positive.

I don't know how famous we'll be. I can only hope that we will be remembered for our words. Kellie Frasier said, "If we live by the example of our words, then others will know it is possible. It'll give them the credibility they need to be effective in their relationships and lives." To me, that means that we have to practice what we preach. But when we preach, we have to assemble the right words and express them eloquently so that people will remember them. And why do we want to be remembered? Because we want to know that we made a difference. That is why, while fame might be the goal, the driving force should be impact. So let's creatively compose and convey our very own powerful words to induce change. And let's leave our signature on the ears of all who will listen. And in the namesake of the website, Words That Shook The World, let's shake the world with our words. Those have been my words to you....Have a Safe, Pleasant, and Positive Day!

So it's no surprise that I love public speaking. But whether or not you share my passion, one thing we do share is the power of our words…from the points of our pens to the tips of our tongues…whether it be in front of a large audience, in the comfort of our homes, or at the place where we work…whether it be on a dinner date, at the bar with our friends, or on the playground with our kids…we all have something of value to say, something to be remembered by.

"Have a Safe, Pleasant, and Positive Day!"

BEYOND LIMITATIONS

Quote: "If you think you are perfect, then you have room for improvement."

Sometimes we just have to sit back and reflect and think about why it is that we are not where we want to be.

The fact of the matter is this: sometimes, it's not because we didn't show the initiative to start on that path. And sometimes, it's not because we didn't show the determination to drive us towards that goal. And sometimes, it's not because we didn't work hard enough in our attempts to accomplish that goal.

In fact, sometimes, we do all of that, but we still find ourselves falling short. And that's because sometimes, we forget one of the essentials of success: we have to evolve.

There I was sitting in the audience, waiting to take the stage for the third round of the World Championship of Public Speaking Contest. Minutes before my speech, as I watched the speaker who would eventually take first to my second place, I suddenly realized that I had forgotten my prop.

Where was my focus?

I don't know what was occupying my thoughts, but at least I remembered to gather my prop before I spoke. But it didn't matter because once I began to speak, I began to forget my words. As a matter of fact, I left out an entire section. I don't think most people even noticed. But of course they didn't, because they had never heard the speech. But I knew of course, because I had practiced those same exact words a million times. I had advanced past rounds one and two with those same exact words.

So what happened? After all, isn't it true that "Practice makes Perfect"? Not quite. And that was the problem. Not that I didn't practice, but that I hadn't perfected. And while I know that delivery always needs to be practiced, I also realized, later, that the presentation always needs to be perfected, constantly.

When I first composed that speech, I was so proud of it. When I first practiced it, I was so excited. The words were fresh in my mind. The words were new to me.

BEYOND LIMITATIONS

But as time progressed, I didn't practice those words as much as I should have. Or rather, when I did practice, I practiced the same exact words. And the truth is, I got bored with the speech. It became stale for me. It became too much of a routine for me. The excitement was gone. Complacency had festered. And so while I was prepared to present what I believed to be my best work, I hadn't truly prepared to be my best.

Sometimes I think that we either fall victim to the belief that we have truly prepared ourselves to be the best or that we fall victim to a false sense of what our best can be.

Regardless, whatever we believe our best to be, we should strive to be better. What's better than your best? That depends on how you redefine your best. I met a mother after one of my talks about effective study habits. She said she struggles to motivate her son because he believes that he does not need to work harder. He's getting good grades with little effort. When I asked her what his good grades are. She said, "He gets 85s, but I want him to do better." She said that she tells him that 85 is mediocre. He says that he disagrees. So who's right? It's not really a matter of right or wrong? It's a matter of definition and redefinition. Once he changes his definition of "good grades", he will change his effort to meet his definition. He will change how he prepares to be his best.

I didn't follow my own motto: "Your Performance is only as Great as your Preparation." My preparation was far from great and nowhere near perfect. And that again was the problem.

In my head for some reason I thought that I had achieved a level of perfection. I had composed the perfect speech. Perfect? What does it mean to be perfect? It means that something is flawless; it requires nothing else because it can get no better. I had written the perfect speech, or had I? Of course not. Let's face it; there's no such thing. Nothing and no one is perfect because perfection is unattainable. What I call "perfection" is a level of comfort. Sometimes, we are comfortable at a peak we've reached. Whether we are comfortable at a level of mediocrity or greatness, it doesn't matter because it's not the level of success, but rather the level of comfort that holds us back or prevents us from getting better. We need to evolve because if we think what we do is perfect, then we have room for improvement.

BEYOND LIMITATIONS

I should have revised my speech. Through the duration of three rounds, the equivalent of several weeks, I should have made changes to the speech. After all, I teach students that writing is a process. There is no such thing as a final draft. There is just a recent draft that we decide to submit for the last time. But what we produce can always be better.

No wonder I lost my focus...I kept everything the same. I never revised the speech. I never evolved the presentation. I got comfortable with what worked. Now, I can't say, that if I had made changes to the speech that I would have placed first. After all, the first place winner wrote a great speech. But evolving my practice has less to do with the results of a competition or the definition of what others perceive as the best, and more about getting better, not necessarily perfect, at what I do.

But I do advise my first place counterpart to put his speech through the process of evolution as he prepares for Round 5 and hopefully Round 6, the final round.

Without change, we get complacent.

Without change, we get bored.

Without change, we don't progress.

And I want to progress. I'm sure that we all do.

I'm already contemplating what my speech entry will be for next year's competition. And I plan to make changes periodically, before the competition, and if I advance, throughout the competition.

Perfection is a funny thing because it's unattainable and yet we're encouraged to strive for it. So we can't get discouraged when we don't achieve it. And we can never embrace it when we foolishly think we achieve it. Perfection must always be a goal, but it must never be the end. Remember what Laurence Miller said: "Excellence is not an accomplishment. It's a spirit...a never-ending process."

So strive for perfection. And when you reach it, keep going.

There's no room for comfort, but there's always room for improvement.

BEYOND LIMITATIONS

Quote: " If we want to do it, we can. The only failure is not to try, because putting forth the effort is success in itself."
                                        -Sister Madonna Buder

So I was watching this special on NBCSports about the Triathlon. I love watching those videos. I wish I could compete in the triathlon. It's not the physical strength or the endurance that stops me. It's the swimming. If I ever want to pursue that dream, I have to work on that.

But I don't watch these clips for training purposes. I watch them for inspiration. First of all, the feat is amazing. And the effort is even more amazing. The sheer willingness is inspiring.

The Ironman Triathlon involves a 2.4-mile swim, a 112-mile bike ride, and a full marathon: 26.2 miles. That's insane. And that's why I love watching it.

To see the winner cross that finish line shows that with enough preparation, you can be the best. As I like to say, "Your performance is only as great as your preparation."

But the true glory of this event doesn't lie in the win, but rather, in the finish.

I watched one woman will her body towards the finish line as the clock approached the 12-hour mark. If you don't cross the finish line by the 12th hour, you don't go down in the record books as finishing the race. Can you imagine how that must feel after all the blood, sweat, and tears?

Four seconds after the 12th hour, the mother crossed the finish line.

BEYOND LIMITATIONS

Four seconds.

But the tears she cried must have been from the sight of her daughters who were so proud of their mother. Forget the four seconds. It's the finish that is phenomenal.

And then I watched the image of a man who lied on his back, exhausted, broken, but vowing to return one day to complete his unfinished business. Even those who don't finish inspire us with their effort and their desire to try again.

And then there was the 52-year old doctor who collapsed several times, only to rise again to make it to the finish line, the final collapse into his family's arms. He did it. And he would write his own prescription: rest for the next few days.

I took to the Internet briefly to see other stories, like the one about the two women, bodies broken, spirits alive, who were racing for 4th place. Neither could hold up their bodies any longer. So they crawled. Who cares who got fourth or fifth place? One pulled the other across the finish line. The feat of the finish outweighs the thrill of the victory.

As I pulled myself back to the television, I saw the blood crawl down the side of her face. But she was determined. Nothing would stop her. Nothing did stop her. Sacrifice is the price of success.

Upon watching this, I remembered mentoring a student who had cut class for 30 days and told me that he could never return because he was afraid to face his teachers and because he had fallen so far behind that he believed that he couldn't bring himself to even try. I found an article for him to read about a tri-athlete who had been hospitalized after a nearly fatal car accident, and who had been told that he would never walk again.

BEYOND LIMITATIONS

He crossed that finish line. If he could do that, then that kid could do what he needed to do.

It was a long article, so I don't know if the student read it. But if I ever meet him again, or when I have the opportunity to mentor another kid, I will surely show them the footage of the triathlon that I watched. It can bring tears to your eyes. It can fire you up, especially the story about Sister Madonna Buder.

Her nickname is the Iron Nun. At 81 years old and nearly 300 triathlons under her belt since the age of 55, she is a true inspiration. I read an article about her that closed with these words:

"First, you have to have the desire. Then, once you have the desire, you can become a little bit more daring, and with daring you get determination. And with determination comes the dedication, and then the actual doing. Those are the five Ds."

And then she told the reporter Mark Hertz, "If we want to do it, we can. The only failure is not to try, because putting forth the effort is success in itself."

I would love to compete in a triathlon and become an Ironman, but that's not why I wrote this.

I wrote this because it's inspiring.

It motivates me.

It tells me that I, we, can do it, whatever it is that we want to do.

We can do it.

If we have the will, then we have **the winner's** spirit.

So go after what you want. And finish!

BEYOND LIMITATIONS

Quote: "Endurance is not just the ability to bear a hard thing, but to turn it into glory." -William Barclay

In March 2012, I delivered the following speech for all of us who need the inspiration to keep going regardless of the struggles that stand in our way.

"I want to dedicate this speech to a young man from my school who passed away because of a brain tumor. In his last few months, he was in no condition to come to school. He could barely walk down the hall without leaning against the wall. His parents had to arrange for a car service to pick him up and take him home every day. As I understand it, his parents begged him not to go to school anymore. But he just would not quit. I admire that. And I wish he were here so I could ask him, "What keeps you going?" But instead, I asked myself that very question: "What keeps me going?" "What keeps us going?" That's a great question because let's face it: life is hard. And when life is not beating you down, life is standing in your way. And yet, we still do it. We fall off that horse and we get back up. We figure out what we need to do and then we do things like join Toastmasters, break the ice with our first speech, and stand in front of an audience delivering a tenth speech, minutes before becoming a Competent Communicator, en route to be becoming a Distinguished Toastmaster.

By the way, do you know why I'm here…because someone cancelled out. About two years ago, the Assistant Principal of Guidance at my school told me that she was running a meeting for 64 young men who needed Motivation…Inspiration. But her guest speaker cancelled out. And so she asked me to speak. And I said yes, but the truth is I had no idea what I would say to these young men. But then it dawned on me. She said, "Marc, you're a role model." Now maybe I was too humble to agree with her, but I appreciate that she said that because it gave me an idea for what to say. That night, I didn't talk about what I had done. Instead, I talked about What Keeps Me Going.

BEYOND LIMITATIONS

What Keeps Me Going? I'll tell you what keeps me going:

- The belief that there isn't anything that I can't do
- The belief that any obstacle, any challenge in life is not a source of frustration, but rather a source of motivation
- The understanding that the things we want most in life take time to acquire
- The understanding that success is a product of a purpose, a passion, and a plan

Now that all sounds nice, but I have often found that after all the positive and motivational messages, what we need is some solid advice. After all, whenever we don't feel like going on anymore, it's usually because we don't know what else to do.

So I read an article on Pickyourbrain.com that said we should reach out to experts. There is always someone else who has done what you are trying to do. And this person can tell you the next step to take. Josh Shipp is a professional speaker for young audiences. I got an email from him that said don't wait for the opportunity. Create the opportunity. So I took his advice. I found the emails of all the school principals in New York City and I am sending them emails asking if they are looking for a guest speaker. That's how one parent coordinator got my email. Good advice.

I watched a DVD about becoming a professional speaker. The presenter said when you figure out what you want to do, dedicate a set amount of time per week to work on your task. Nothing in life is guaranteed, but you are guaranteed nothing if you don't put in the time and the work.

Finally, constantly remind yourself why you are doing what you are doing. Often, we get sidetracked. Often, we forget. But every single time, we are inspired, by someone or something.

I started by saying that I want to dedicate this speech to that young man from my school…because he inspired me. He inspired me to ask myself that question, "What Keeps Me Going?" He inspired me to deliver this message to you. And he inspired me to find a quote that sums this all up: Vivian Komori said, "Life is not about how fast you run. Life is not about how high you climb. Life is about how well you bounce."

BEYOND LIMITATIONS

Quote: *"Sometimes, the opportunity we want is not the opportunity we get. But any opportunity is a chance to create a moment."*

Good evening and Congratulations to the Class of 2012! My name is Mr. Williams. And it is with great sincerity that I wish for all of you....A Safe, Pleasant, and Positive Future!

And it is with great pleasure that I stand before you to honor one of your classmates, a classmate who is deserving of an award for all of her hard work and dedication to support, organize, and contribute to so many student activities over the course of her four years at the school. And as I tell you a few reasons why I think your classmate is so amazing, I want to take this same opportunity to give you some advice.

When she came to the school four years ago, she joined the Student Council. Now that may not be a point of interest for many people and it doesn't have to be. After all, not everyone is into politics. But after knowing her for so long, I can say with confidence that she didn't join Student Council because of politics. And she didn't join to enhance her high school profile for college. She joined so that she could serve, contribute to, and impact her school: the population, the environment, the community. And I admire that; I admire her heart because it is dedicated to others.

And that's a lesson we can all learn from. In life, you will do a lot of things for yourself. And that's okay. But as you pursue your professional goals, don't look for what others can do for you, but rather, look for what you can do for others. Think about it: the late, great Steve Jobs was not successful because he made a lot of money. He was successful because he was good at figuring out what people wanted and he figured out ways to give it to them.

Actually, an article I read recently about Steve Jobs said that he didn't believe in giving people what they wanted because by the time you can give them what they want, they will want something new. "He told Inc. magazine in 1989, "You can't just ask customers what they want and then try to give that to them. By the time you get it built, they'll want something

new." So in actuality, here's what made Steve Jobs a success: he gave people what they wanted way before they knew they wanted it.

"A reporter who asked Jobs about the market research that went into the iPad was famously told, "None. It's not the consumers' job to know what they want. Which isn't to say that he doesn't think like a consumer--he just thinks like one standing in the near future, not in the recent past. He is a focus group of one, the ideal Apple customer, two years out."

He was a visionary; it's true. The future needs more visionaries with a pulse on what people need.

It's your turn to create a vision for a new generation.

Now let me bring your attention back to your classmate. Two years ago, I was assigned to supervise a summer program. And she chose to come in every day to help: no paycheck, no volunteer hours, no A/C; it was brutal that summer. There were seemingly no benefits to coming in to help me out, but she came in to help anyway.

She assessed my office, my files, and my records. She completely reorganized everything. She had taken a task I had never done before and turned it into a task I would adopt and continue to practice. She made me more effective, just like she made Student Council more effective, just like she made the operations of student activities more effective…because her organizational skills are phenomenal. And this is something we can learn from.

Essential to your professional success and leadership is organization. When we're organized, we build confidence in ourselves and give ourselves direction. And in turn, we do the same for those we lead. So walk into every situation with a plan for how to do what you want to do, and you will find that you will do it effectively.

Finally, no matter the time, every time I turned around she was working on something for the school. Every project that had to be completed, she was working on it. Every chance there was to attend a leadership conference, she tried to go, and even when she couldn't attend, she persisted until she could. And when Student Council wasn't enough, she joined another school leadership organization. And in addition to surrounding herself with good friends and positive people, she took it upon herself to do something that was incredibly instrumental to her growth as a leader: she found herself a mentor. And we can learn a lesson from this in particular.

Whatever it is you are going to do that you are good at doing, just remember that you can always get better. And the best way to get better is to find someone who will give you the advice you want and the feedback that you may not want. I love the quote, " Most people seldom improve when they have no other models but themselves to copy." Consider this: Donald Trump is a symbol of success in our society and a mentor to many. But it is very well documented that he would not be where he is today if he did not find his mentor: George Ross.

"It's not just winners of the TV show "The Apprentice" who can benefit from the guidance of a mentor. Learning from someone with more professional experience than you can give you access to their accumulated wisdom, and allow you to learn from their mistakes.

The ideal mentor is someone who you respect, can connect with on a personal level, and who is willing to impart his or her knowledge. But don't expect them to solve all your problems.

Professor David Megginson, of Sheffield Hallam University, says a mentor's role is to help you to make sense of your own experiences.

"What's useful in mentoring is the opportunity to think through your own issues and what you want to do about them with somebody who has an understanding of your sector, or thinking about the kind of challenges you're going to face in the role you have." (Mark Tutton, CNN reporter).

I could go on highlighting the qualities of your classmate from whom we can learn a lot of lessons, but I'll close with this...

BEYOND LIMITATIONS

I then added my closing remarks and sat down. I had just finished presenting an award to one of the graduating seniors. I was one of several speakers that day, none of which were the keynote speaker. I would have loved to have delivered the keynote address, but it wasn't meant to be....well sort of...

After a long journey to find a keynote speaker for the 2012 graduation ceremony, the graduation committee found themselves without anyone who could share any words of wisdom that would send the class off from high school and into the world of higher education and the professional world. When they first approached me about suggestions for a keynote, I had suggested they reach out to a few speaker bureaus. What they found were prohibitive costs that the class simply could not afford. And though I had offered to speak myself, they let me down easy, letting me know that what they wanted was someone famous. I understand. Who doesn't want that "wow" factor? Jaws dropping; eyes popping; cameras flashing, texts sending: that's the memory they wanted. And bless their hearts; they worked towards it. Imagine the excitement when they received a reply to a request to get an A-List celebrity to deliver the commencement speech! But one thing prevented the "wow" moment: the price tag was larger than any speaker from the bureaus I had suggested. Big dreams! Big money! Big letdown. And unfortunately, time had run out. There was no longer enough time to book someone because the ceremony was two weeks away. Then I received this email asking me to deliver the keynote address. But shortly after, they said, "We're sorry, but we no longer have room on the program for a keynote, but we would like you to present an award in honor of one of our graduates." I thought about it. And then I said yes.

Sometimes, the opportunity we want is not the opportunity we get. But any opportunity is a chance to create a moment.

Seize your opportunity!

Create your moment!

BEYOND LIMITATIONS

Quote: " There is no such thing as destiny. The only thing that exists is a destination. And the only way to reach your destination is through initiative, hard work, and determination. "

One day, my neighbor's son told me that he didn't believe he needed to work hard because in life, there is a balance: for every bad thing that happens, a good thing happens. That's why he wasn't worried about failing English, which would jeopardize his chances of graduating from high school. It didn't matter, because he was sure that he was destined for greatness.

He's gonna be a rock star.

When I asked him for evidence of this balance in life that he called destiny, he said that after his friend was in a car accident, his friend got a new car. When he said that, I couldn't help but hear in the back of my head the words of Cliff Huxtable, who, in response to his son's impassioned speech about, "Why can't you just love me for who I am?" said, "That's the dumbest thing I ever heard. No wonder you get D's". (If you've never seen the episode, I highly recommend it).

But I digress. I heard those words but didn't repeat them. What I should've said was that his example was not a sign of some balance in life, that for every bad event, there's a good one. That's just simply a matter of a bad occurrence followed by the benefit of having parents (or a lawyer) who work hard for their money. Now granted, I don't know his friend, his friend's parents, or their lawyer (if they even have one). But I don't need to know them to know this:

If you think you don't have to work hard in life to get what you want because you are destined for greatness or at least destined to live the good life, then let me break it down for you.

In life, there is no destiny. There is only a destination. And the best way to reach your destination is through initiative, determination, and hard work.

I was watching the news one day and saw a feature about the huge lottery jackpot that had everyone in a craze. I don't even play lotto, but I contributed my dollars, for days, to the office pool. The resident expert on playing lotto was interviewed for the story and advised us all not to let the machine randomly select numbers for us. It's best to strategically choose our own numbers. Look at that, even in a game of chance, the best tip is not to leave our destination in the hands of destiny.

But I don't think the kid is a believer yet. Actually, let me rephrase that, he is still a believer, in destiny that is. After all, he failed the class, got transferred to a new class (not because his failure was a testament of his refusal to work hard, but rather because of the fate that placed him in the class of a really tough teacher who just graded too hard and had it out for him). Now he's passing. So, some would say, maybe that first teacher was too tough. I don't think so, but that's not the point. The issue moving forward for this kid is that if he does indeed graduate on time, he might continue to live his life thinking that he can just sit back and let life happen. He'll just endure the bad and wait for the good, and hopefully not end up in the ugly. But if he truly aspires to be that rock star, then his rock star mentality needs to change.

In order to be a star, you can't let the stars fall where they may. You have to plant your feet into the ground to solidify that star on the walk of fame.

After all, metaphorically speaking of course, isn't that the goal: not to settle to be just another star in the sky?

You wanna be a star: aspire to be the sun.

Isn't the goal not to just pass the class, but to pass with flying colors?

Isn't the goal not to just graduate, but to graduate with honors?

Isn't the goal to not just live the good life, but to live great?

Like most people, this kid obviously does have a goal, but he just had the wrong mentality. And he won't get to where he wants to go until he changes his mind or benefits from the hard work of others, whether it be his parents, his lawyer, or his band mates. And success on the backs of others is not success. It's just life in the shadow of success.

Speaking of bandmates, I have to also share that this kid's other evidence of the balance in life was the lead singer of Slipknot. He said that the lead singer didn't even graduate from high school, but look at him

BEYOND LIMITATIONS

now. I figured if this is his role model, the proof he was going to use, his justification for coasting through life until destiny delivers greatness directly to him, then I wanted to learn more about this lead singer. What's his name?" I asked. He said he didn't know. How are you going to use someone as a model for your behavior if you don't even know the guy's name? He said that the band members purposely use stage names, so no one knows their real names.

Fact check: all I did was Google lead singer of Slipknot. The first thing that pops up is Corey Taylor on Wikipedia. I won't report to you all that I found, but I'll share this much from the Corey Taylor page on a Slipknot website.

What was high school like? "I got kicked out, basically, my junior year I started a riot in the lunch room, because of the atrocious food. They kindly asked me to leave and I threw a chair at the vice principal."

When did you start out with music? "The first live gig I ever did was actually with Stone Sour. This was in '92. I was 19 years old and I was so nervous man. We would do originals and covers and we would play three one-hour sets a night. We would do that four or five days a week. It kind of taught you a work ethic, you know?"

Conclusion: Yes, Corey Taylor is a success. I'd be misleading you if I didn't acknowledge that. And he should be applauded for making it out of the hole he seemingly dug himself into, both before and even during his successful run. But the key point is that he dug himself into that hole. He is accountable. And my neighbor's son needs to understand that failing English or not graduating high school on time would be the fault of no one or nothing else but himself, not any teacher and not any destiny.

We've all heard the quote, "You control your own destiny." The key word is not "destiny". The key words are "you control". Translation: You have to work hard for everything you want. Sorry, I must correct myself. You must work hard for everything. Whether you want something or not, you have to work hard because success is not achieved through an isolated effort of working hard. Success is achieved through a habit of working hard.

BEYOND LIMITATIONS

Think about what Corey Taylor eventually learned: *"We would do originals and covers and we would play three one-hour sets a night. We would do that four or five days a week. It kind of taught you a work ethic, you know?"* He learned a work ethic.

In essence, he learned that there is no such thing as destiny. The only thing that exists is a destination. And the only way to reach your destination is through initiative, determination, and hard work.

When I was in college, I wanted to be a host on the college radio station. That was an early indication that I wanted to use my voice professionally.

Initiative: I went to the studio and inquired about how I could get on the air and host my own show. I got the paperwork, which included an application and notes for a test I would have to take. Yes, a test...they can't just let anyone at the controls.

I studied. That was my determination.

I passed the test. That was my success.

Well, that was a success on a long road that I unfortunately wasn't willing to work hard enough for to achieve. After the written test, applicants had to learn some of the technical aspects of the trade, like handling the reel-to-reel. But my attitude was that I didn't want to do that. I just wanted to speak on the radio, play songs, and entertain my listeners. Didn't they have somebody to do the tech work? A foolish attitude meant that I was unwilling to put in the work. Of course, now I understand that the more you know about your trade, your practice, your hobby, your profession (you get the idea) the better you are at what you do and the more marketable you are when you are ready to step onto a larger stage.

I love talking in metaphors, but let me break that down differently: learn as much as you can about what you do; your goal should be to become the expert in your area, not a person limited by what you limit yourself to be.

Who knows: I could have been Ryan Seacrest by now. Maybe I could have been that guy with shows airing in multiple cities by now. Maybe I could have been the rock star of radio by now. Some would say, "Maybe it wasn't meant to be." I say that's incorrect. What is meant to be usually refers to what is destined to be. What happened to me is that "It didn't work out for me because I didn't work for it."

I showed the initiative. I showed the determination...well at least I showed determination initially. And I even put in a little work at first, but ultimately, I didn't work hard, not hard enough. It's a simple equation for success. And we have to be willing to put it all together. And if by chance we don't, then we have to be honest with ourselves that it's not the forces of nature that are working against us; sometimes, that force is us. And there's no balance that will save us, unless it's a balance of initiative, determination, and hard work.

In closing, here's my disclaimer. This is not a religious statement. There's no comment here about an almighty plan or a divine power. Even if there is a plan, we are the ones who choose the path. And if we don't follow the path of Initiative, Determination, and Hard work, then the destiny we choose will be nothing but a dead end.

So don't go for the dead end.

Go for the destination.

And always remember that you need the "drive" to get there.

BEYOND LIMITATIONS

Dream. Pursue. Achieve

"A good idea alone is not enough. Ever. It takes action, it takes a strategy and it takes hard work to turn a good idea into a great one. Don't ever stop with a good idea. Work hard to turn your good ideas into gold." -Cathey Armillas

For the last year and a half, I've been pursuing a career as a professional speaker, not only because I have a passion to mentor people in their pursuit to be more productive and successful, not only because I have a passion to motivate and inspire people to rise beyond their everyday struggles to chase and reach their dreams, but also because I love public speaking.

I'll say that again...I love public speaking!

There aren't many people who can say that.

Most people feel the exact opposite. Jerry Seinfeld once said that because people are so afraid to speak in public, if most people were asked to speak at a funeral, they would rather be in the casket. Now obviously that's a gross exaggeration, but there's a great amount of truth in that statement about how uncomfortable people are with public speaking.

So I had an idea.

I want to motivate and help as many people as I can, whether they are afraid to speak in public or they just want to improve their public speaking skills; I want to help people not only step in front of a room and take the stage, but to step up in front of a room and "command" the stage.

That's my idea.

But as my good friend Cathey Armillas said, "A good idea alone is not enough. Ever. It takes action, it takes a strategy and it takes hard work to turn a good idea into a great one. Don't ever stop with a good idea. Work hard to turn your good ideas into gold."

143

BEYOND LIMITATIONS

So I turned my idea into a presentation. And maybe one day a book will follow. My seminar outlines what I like to call…

"The Rules of E.N.G.A.G.E.M.EN.T."

It started when I crafted the presentation for a leadership conference at my high school. Then I repackaged it and delivered it at a Regional Conference for the National Society of Black Engineers. And in February 2013, I shared my "rules" at the PACE University Annual Student Leadership Conference. And one student approached me immediately after the presentation, and said that she had just been offered the position as the president of her club but she turned down the offer because she's afraid to speak in public. Then she told me that my "talk" motivated her; she now sees the difference public speaking can make and how she can benefit from being a better public speaker. And now she plans to accept the offer to be the president of her club.

My idea has become an action.
And my action has inspired others to action.

But I have some more work to do as I attempt to spin this idea into gold because each time I deliver the presentation, I have more to share than the time allows. That's why I am working on the book.

But before you and others read what I intend to be my next book, I just want to admit that I thought about just posting the rules without all this extra commentary, but I always like to embrace the opportunity to motivate people to take their passions and their dreams and create a plan to achieve whatever it is you desire.

Dream. Pursue. Achieve.

BEYOND LIMITATIONS

The Black Belt and Beyond

Last Saturday night, I saw three young boys: two 11 year-olds and one 12 year-old, dig deeper than I have ever seen most people dig before. For the first time in my life, I saw a black belt exam. And it was grueling.

I witnessed these three boys endure drill after drill after drill after drill. They ran lap after lap after lap and performed kicks, and then punches, and then strikes, and then ran more laps.

I saw them drop to the floor and do push-up after push-up after push-up. Then they persisted through defensive drills of being choked and attacked by a mob of the sensei's assistants. These three boys were exhausted. I could see them getting weak. And then the sensei instructed them to perform 1000 jumping jacks....surely that was just a metaphor. When they reached 90, I was sure they would stop. But it was when they reached 990 consecutive jumping jacks that I realized this was for real.

I could not believe what I was seeing. And keep in mind; I was an hour late. And they weren't even half way through the torture. But the part that astounded me the most was the sparring session. Each kid padded up and then proceeded to spar against a gauntlet of ten other students. Each and every time, by the time one of the boys reached the 8th sparring partner, he would stop fighting. I could see that they wanted to quit.

I could see it in their eyes, in their tears.
I could see it as they clutched their chests in pain.
I could see it as the fell to their knees.

But as they lay on the brink of exhaustion and defeat, the sensei would grab each by his head. And without raising his voice, he would blast some stern words into the boy's face. And then he would say loud enough for the crowd of tearful mothers, worried fathers, and fearful families and friends to hear, "This doesn't end until I see you fight back...until you fight strong!"

BEYOND LIMITATIONS

Each time, each kid found something deep inside to persist. The sensei would yell, "What does it mean to persist?!" And everyone in the room responded, "It means to never give up!" Our hands thundered together to rally each kid back to his feet. We believed each of them could persist and persist strongly.

I was inspired.
And when the sparring was done, the sensei ordered them to do more calisthenics.

Whatever I struggle with from this moment forward, I will envision these three boys and their strength, their persistence, their commitment.

I was invited to speak to them and their families after the exam, to motivate them to take the lessons from a 4-year journey to earn a black belt and use those lessons to achieve all their aspirations in life.

I walked in to motivate them, but I was the one who was inspired.
And here is what I was inspired to say…
"Good evening everyone. My name is Marc Williams. And first I want to tell you that I am honored to be here with you tonight and I want to thank Rean for inviting me because I love celebrating success and learning from success.

And one thing that I want to share with you about success was written by Alex Noble who once said, "Success is not defined by the place where you are, but instead, success is defined by the spirit with which you undertake and continue your journey.

And it's that journey that I want to talk about tonight. Because even though I was never a student of the martial arts, one thing that I've come to learn, appreciate, and respect about the martial arts is the journey that you have to take, like the one from white belt, to yellow, to orange, to blue, to purple, to green, to brown...to the black belt.

BEYOND LIMITATIONS

Give yourselves a round of applause if you are earning your black belt tonight. Congratulations. And to anyone who may not earn their black belt or for that matter not achieve a particular goal when you wish to achieve it (and that's everyone by the way), just remember that if from your experience you learned the four essential principles of success, then your success is not defined by a deadline; your success is simply a matter of time.

And it is from that experience that you should have learned those four principles: always set goals, always practice discipline, always endure and persist beyond any struggle, and always work hard. I read an article the other day about what it means to earn a black belt and the author said that earning a black belt means absolutely nothing...if you only do it to get the belt, if you only do it to learn to fight, or if you only do it to compete, because the true value in earning a black belt is in the ability to walk away with those four principles that have helped you succeed to this point and will help you succeed beyond this point as you continue your journey.

Now along that journey, you all walked into karate school, many of you with the goal of becoming a black belt. And then you probably learned pretty quickly that in order to achieve your goals, you have to take the necessary steps. And then you probably learned that you have to change your perception so you can understand that every step along the way is in actuality a goal in itself.

And that's when you probably learned that you must always set goals because success is not about achieving a goal; success is about creating a habit of achieving goal after goal after goal.

And as you reach for the next goal, it must be a greater challenge because as Michaelangelo said, "The greatest danger for most of us is not that we aim too high and miss the mark but that we aim too low and reach it."

And as we set these goals, let's remember a few tips: 1) Always be realistic; I always tell everybody that I believe that we can do anything we want to do, but we must first develop the skills to do it. 2) Tell somebody about your goal; there 's something about putting it out in public that

BEYOND LIMITATIONS

pushes us. One day, I told a friend that my goal was to finish the first draft of my book before the end of the summer. The very next day, I started working harder than I had ever done before and I finished the first draft two weeks ago. *(By the way, I know I said earlier that we should wait before we tell others about our goals and I stand by that. So for the purposes of clarity, allow me to explain. We shouldn't wait until after we have accomplished the goal before we tell someone about what we aimed to accomplish. Instead, we should wait until after we've gotten started and gained some confidence in whatever it is we are trying to do. Notice my example: I started my draft well before telling anyone that I wanted to write a book, and then after I was nearly done, I began to share my project with my family and friends.)* 3) Finally, don't be afraid of failure because failure is just a part of the process. The most successful people in the world have failed more times than they will ever succeed and that is why they are successful.

So set your goals and aim high, and when you reach your goals, then go higher as you continue your journey.

Now somewhere along the journey, you will feel weak. We all do. And somewhere along the journey, you will feel lazy. We all do. Let's be honest, how many times did you not feel like coming to class because you were just too tired? And how many times did you get pushed down so hard that you started to second guess whether or not you wanted to come back to class? That's when we need discipline the most.

Always practice discipline because the straightest path to success is paved by the focus, the commitment, and the consistency you need not to steer away from or be drawn from your course.
I read an article recently about how many people earn their black belt. And the studies show that only a little less than 3 percent of the people who try to earn their black belt actually do it. Most people never make it past the orange belt. And as people move higher, only about half of any group makes it to the next level. And when asked what makes the final group continue their journey, the answer is choice.

BEYOND LIMITATIONS

Disciple is about choice, the same choice I am personally faced with when I stand in front of a vending machine. I know that I should choose the water instead of the soda.

When I pick the soda, I'm being weak. When I choose the water, I'm practicing discipline. And when I wanted to join the wrestling team in college and the coach picked the smallest guy on the team for me to spar with, I never went back because I lacked the commitment. Yes, the smallest guy on the team did tie me in a knot, but what prevented me from coming back was my lack of commitment.

But you know who does have commitment? Sarah Robles is the strongest women in the United States. She is a female weightlifter who competed in the 2012 Olympics. But she almost didn't make it to the Olympics because she couldn't afford to train. She only made $400 a month. She barely could afford to eat what weightlifters need to eat in order to compete. She could barely afford to train with her coach because she didn't have the gas money. Some days, she would just put $2.00 in the tank just to make it to the gym. And then, she'd put another $2.00 in the tank to make it home. And though, she struggled, she made it work because she was committed to her dream. And though she didn't bring home any medals, she has been approached by several sponsors who will support her as she prepares for the 2016 Olympics. Such is the reward one is likely to receive when others see the commitment we have to our journey.

But just remember that like setting goals, discipline is also a habit, one that needs to be exercised. Just like athletes exercise their muscles, we must exercise our discipline.

Every day we are faced with a choice, something we want to do but know we shouldn't and something we'd rather not do but know we should. Starting tomorrow, just once a day, choose something you'd rather not do. When you get home, do the dishes before you take out a new plate, turn on the news before you turn on a video game or your favorite TV show. Drink that water before you choose the soda. Start with the small and easy choices. You will be building a habit that will help you when you have to make the harder choices.

Exercise your discipline and you will find the greatest success along your journey.

And something else you will find along your journey is something I talked about earlier: failure. Like I said, failure is a part of the process. There is no success without failure. And we have to understand that if we are mentally prepared for failure, then failure won't do to us what it has done to so many others.

Failure can break you.
Failure can break your spirit and your confidence.
And failure can alter the course of your journey if you let it.

Just remember that your ability to endure and persist is planted in your mentality and your perception. I actually don't use the word failure. I call it a struggle. Maybe it's just a word, but it works for me because I'm inspired by the many people who have overcome their struggles.

Mantel Mitchell is a runner on the U.S.A. Olympic track team, the same team that won a silver medal in 2012. But they would not have done it, had it not been for him. During his first leg of the race, he heard a snap. His leg actually broke while he was running, but he never stopped running. He made it to the next runner, and as I said before, his team went on to the finals where they won the silver medal. And when asked what motivated him to keep running, he said, "Three things: faith, focus and finish." He had the faith that he could make it. He focused, not on the pain, but on the goal. And his goal was to finish, and that's what he did.

We can endure and persist through any struggle. Only our mentality can draw us from our course, or more importantly, can keep us on our course.

So exercise your mentality and always dig deep to find the spirit and courage you need to overcome any obstacle that lies on the road along your journey. Endurance and persistence can drive you through those walls.

BEYOND LIMITATIONS

"Success seems to be largely a matter of hanging on after others have let go." -William Feather

"Don't let the fear of the time it will take to accomplish something stand in the way of your doing it. The time will pass anyway; we might just as well put that passing time to the best possible use." -Earl Nightingale

"Now if you are going to win any battle you have to do one thing. You have to make the mind run the body. Never let the body tell the mind what to do. The body will always give up. It is always tired in the morning, noon, and night. But the body is never tired if the mind is not tired." -George S. Patton, U.S. Army General, 1912 Olympian

And the other thing that will drive you through those walls is hard work. Hard work is what brought you here today. And along your journey, I'm sure that you learned that no one is going to make it easy for you.

If you want it, then you have to work hard to get. I used to tell my students all the time that you must work hard for everything you want. And there is no better example of that that Sister Madonna Buder. If you don't know who she is, they also call her the Iron Nun because at the age of 81, she just competed in the Iron Man triathlon: The Iron Man! That's a 2.4-mile swim followed by a 112-mile bike ride, followed by a 26-mile marathon. That's insane. And since the age of 51, Sister Madonna Buder has competed in over 300 triathlons. But forget about the age for a second; for anyone, it takes so much work just to get in shape to compete for such a race. And you have to push your body so hard to cross that finish line. And it takes years, years of hard work.

You can't just decide one day that you want to compete in the triathlon and just go out and do it. And you can't just decide one day that you want to earn a black belt and just go out and do it.

It takes hard work and you always have to work hard because success is failure if it comes without the blood, the sweat, and the tears. But what is the secret to hard work? I think Steve Pavlina said it best

BEYOND LIMITATIONS

when he wrote that we must find a way to enjoy hard work. So many people associate un-pleasurable things with hard work. No one wants to sweat, bleed, or cry. That's why so many people don't exercise; they know it'll make them tired and cause them pain.

That's why you have to ask yourself this question: will the pleasure of getting what you want be greater than the pain that it'll take to get it? If the answer to that is yes, then you will have figured out the secret to hard work: you have to associate hard work with pleasure.

Someone told me the other day that she used to hate running. But then she saw the results after running everyday and now there's nothing else that she'd rather do. She goes on her journey every day.

And you too will go on a journey every day. And as I wrote the other day, your journey must be driven by a dream. And you must refuse not to see that dream become a reality because that is how you will achieve it. I so whole-heartedly believe in the power of motivation, hard work, persistence, and positivity. And I believe that we all possess this power. And all we have to do is exercise that power so that we can achieve whatever it is that we aspire to do. And yes, we should stop along the way, like we are doing tonight to celebrate our victories. And then some time after, we should reflect on the lessons learned on the path to the victory: like always set goals; always practice discipline; always endure and persist beyond the struggles that stand in your way; and always work hard. And then get back up and keep going as you continue your journey because as Ursula Leguin once said, "It is great to have an end to journey towards, but it is the journey that matters in the end."

****

Before I share the final piece of the P.E.P. T.A.L.K., I invite you to bookmark each of the previous twenty-one "words of motivation" and every couple of days, reread any one of them to feed your mind with some positivity!

****

BEYOND LIMITATIONS

The P.E.P T.A.L.K.

Keep your ears plugged into music that produces energy

"Music gives a soul to the universe, wings to the mind, flight to the imagination and life to everything." -Plato

"Music... will help dissolve your perplexities and purify your character and sensibilities, and in time of care and sorrow, will keep a fountain of joy alive in you." -Dietrich Bonhoeffer

Music has been an incredible source of my own personal energy for as long as I can remember.

Being an 80's child, I remember sleeping at night with the radio on. One night, at midnight, I hopped out of bed to the tune of the Miami Sound Machine's "Conga". With an invisible microphone dancing through my fingertips, I gleefully whispered, "Come on shake your body baby do that Conga, Know you can't control yourself any longer, Feel the rhythm of the music getting stronger, Don't you try to fight it 'til you do that Conga beat". I performed a concert that night in my very own room and ignited a level of energy that I recharge every time I put on a pair of headphones or step onto a dance floor.

And as an 80's kid, I remember staying up late to watch Friday Night Videos and Video Music Box. I'm getting goose bumps as I write this. And I'm listening to music as I write this, my feet tapping to the energy. But I digress. Who could sit down as we watched Michael Jackson break up a gang fight with his dance moves in the video "Beat It". There was one move in particular in that video that I will never forget because it was key in breaking my own shell of shyness.

When I was in elementary school, our teachers organized a cultural assembly. I was a part of the African dancers segment. I felt a little weird I must admit, as we danced down the aisle of the auditorium, shirt-less, wearing very short shorts covered by grass belts cut out of construction paper. Nevertheless, when we got to the stage, we performed a number in unison before breaking out into solo moves. I never expected to be a solo dancer, but during a rehearsal, the teacher in charge, who I believe was trying her best to help me become comfortable and confident, asked me to dance to the music by myself. After some trepidation, I broke out a few steps that ended with this backwards snake-like move I saw in the "Beat It" video. And that was all she needed to see. I don't think the moves were spectacular. But I think my shell cracked at that moment. It was a breakthrough. And I have music to thank for it.

And then there was high school. I was still considerably shy and reserved, but participating in the school play gave me the opportunity to dance. The choreographer would put me in the frontline and the other boys would jokingly ask me to stop making them look bad. I enjoyed dancing so much. I enjoyed music so much.

I enjoyed music so much that I would make hundreds of cassette tapes to fill my walk-man with plenty of music regardless of where I traveled. Soon hundreds of cassettes and cass-ingles turned in a collection of CDs that I would carry with me to play on my portable CD player. And eventually that would turn into travelling with three I-pods so that whenever a battery would lose its charge, I had a backup source of rhythmic energy. And as excessive as that might sound, this addiction to music explains a significant portion of my positive attitude.

And between the downfall of the cassette and the rise of the i-pod, I spent endless nights in nightclubs in Manhattan. Dancing from the moment I stepped onto the floor to the moment the lights turned on, I was infused with an unbelievable amount of energy. And it felt great! Whether I was on the floor with my friends, including one of my two best friends, who to this day still feeds off of the adrenaline and dopamine that is released when the music envelopes the dance floor, or when, on that rare occasion, I took to the club by myself, I learned how powerful music can be in its creation of energy, happiness, and positivity.

In the article "Why Your Brain Craves Music, Michael D. Lemonick writes, "*Music triggers activity in the nucleus accumbens, the same brain structure that releases the "pleasure chemical" dopamine. Music also activates the amygdala, which is involved with the processing of emotion, as well as areas of the prefrontal cortex involved in abstract decision-making.*"

Furthermore, according to the authors at Buzzle.com, studies show that *"listening to music elevates our mood. Music creates a steep rise in the levels of serotonin, which has positive influences on the brain cells that control our mood."*

So what tunes are on your playlist?
What do you listen to during exercise?
What songs do you sing in the shower?
What music do you play on your desktop while working at your desk?

I-Heart Radio and Pandora have become my plug-in drugs at the office, especially after I discovered how listening to music increases productivity. I've often asked some of my struggling mentees about the music they listen to, and I'm always surprised to hear that many of them don't listen to music regularly. I urge them to explore and find music they can enjoy. I've shared with parents and students how listening to classical music or even instrumental versions of their favorite music, as long as it's not too loud or fast, has proven to increase concentration, memory, retention, and academic performance. And Tania Gabrielle highlighted in her article *"Why the World's Most Successful People Avoid Negatively Charged Music"*, the studies show that *"people at work who listened to calming, high frequency music increased productivity by 21.3 percent. People listening to a popular commercial radio station improved by 2.4 percent, and those working in silence decreased their performance by 8.3 percent."*

BEYOND LIMITATIONS

Music is an incredible source of energy for everyone.
From the earplugs to the dance floor,
From the download to the concert;
When we tap into the source known to soothe the savage beast
What we explore is a mood changer,
What we discover is a performance enhancer,
What we experience is a difference.
Listen to your music.
Live through your music.
****

The P.E.P. T.A.L.K.

Positivity Exudes Productivity:

Tell yourself positive things
Act in a positive manner
Listen to and read positive messages
Keep your ears plugged into music that produces energy.

We often underestimate or sometimes dismiss the power of the language we speak and the language we receive, but it's time to tap into that power source and do the things that may seem beyond our limits but that are well within our reach.

Conclusion: Rise Beyond

When people ask me, "How do I stay so positive? How do I keep going?", I tell them that it's my mentality that drives my accomplishments.

Whenever I think about the power of a positive mentality and a motivated mind, I think of sports. To this day, I'm still amazed by this home court advantage philosophy and the tradition of having cheerleaders. I find it hard to believe that simply playing on your home court gives you the physical ability to jump higher, run faster, swing harder, throw farther, or kick straighter. It can't be possible that the cheers from the crowd are the physical equivalent to a steroid. They're not...then again. Cheers don't enhance your physical performance; they enhance your mental performance, which then impacts your physical performance. As I've said before, we need to be our own mental cheerleaders!

The summer of 2012 was a fascinating one for me. As I completed the first draft of this book, I attended a few seminars at which I learned quite a bit about how the brain works and how to engage the mind. I read many articles and books about motivated people and the techniques we can use to get and stay motivated. And I watched a close friend change for the better after a tough couple of summer weeks because of the counsel I was able to give him, counsel that was strengthened by my intrinsic motivation, my research, and my passion to help others to Rise Beyond their Struggle. Some of the valuable information I absorbed and will continue to apply for my own self-motivation and in my attempts to motivate others include the following tips from a website called Sources of Insight (http://sourcesofinsight.com/101-ways-to-motivate-yourself-and-others/):

BEYOND LIMITATIONS

Be confident and calm. From the best athletes, to the most successful executives, to the most brilliant poker players, it's the confident and calm that win the game and enjoy the ride. Gaining clarity and bringing a good mental picture into focus of what you want to accomplish is a way to be confident and calm. It's also very motivating.

Build your band of merry men. Robin Hood knew the journey of life was better with his pals that watched his back. Surround yourself with the people that inspire and delight you, wherever you go.

Change the frame, to change your game. Problems aren't problems when you reframe them as challenges. Challenges are opportunities for growth, excellence, and your personal best. One way to always win in a situation is to challenge yourself with this question: If this situation never were to change, what's the one quality you need to make the most of it? Use your growth as a springboard to new heights and a catalyst for change.

Create a wall of inspiration. Put those pictures up that show you the greatest things in life and what's possible. Get those hopes and dreams up on the wall that remind you what's worth fighting for. Put those words on the wall and quotable quotes that fire you up and make you feel alive. Breathe life into your day with a living wall of the best of the best.

Figure out what you want. When you know what you want, that becomes your North Star, guiding light, and ultimate motivator. Clarity helps create confidence in your path, and it helps you focus and direct your action and energy.

Find your "why." When you have a compelling "why," it will inspire you through thick and through thin.

Set a deadline. Knowing when something is due, or setting a deadline, can help you funnel and focus your action and attention. It can also be very motivating when you have a tight deadline, because you know that once it's over, it won't be looming over your head anymore. It's hard to get motivated for things that are due, "whenever."

BEYOND LIMITATIONS

As you might be able to tell, I don't believe that success is guaranteed, nor do I believe that it is promised. I believe that success is pursued. And it is essential to think that way because if you think of success as only a destination and not a pursuit, then you can become a victim of frustration and disappointment when you don't get the results you desire, and as a result you may quit. Remember, quitting is a choice. Therefore, persistence, endurance, the pursuit of a goal, and the embrace of a struggle is a choice. And by choice, I mean it it's a decision of the mind. Don't be defeated by the struggle; don't be defeated by the mind. Embrace the struggle by controlling the mind. There was an old public service announcement that used the line, "A brain is a terrible thing to waste." I'd like to add that a mind is an amazing tool to use. When we use it strategically, we can embrace any struggle and transform it from a source of frustration to a source of motivation. The definition of the mind is "the element or complex of elements in an individual that feels, perceives, thinks, wills, and especially reasons". Author Walter Russell wrote, "Man's actions are a direct result of his thinking. Human beings manufacture their own mental agony", which means we also manufacture our own mental triumph.

"Another way of looking at the mind is looking at the process used to make a decision. Ask yourself if you're making it with your mind or with your heart. Since we can separate feelings from the mind, we can eliminate [self-defeating] emotions that affect our behavior. You can ask yourself what would my mind or sense of logic want me to do and then what does my heart want me to do. Often they are two different decisions or sets of actions. The mind is said to override our emotions, our nervous systems, and most of our physical needs. We can control many functions with our minds." -Mary Kurus

The feelings associated with wanting to quit because of the struggle: anger, hopelessness, depression, frustration, despair are the very emotions that we don't allow our minds to override. It's more natural to give in to those feelings of defeat rather than to create those thoughts of endurance. But I say, don't be a slave to your emotions. Be a master of our mind.

BEYOND LIMITATIONS

"The power of the mind is beyond our imaginations. Since thought always precedes action we come to the conclusion that if we can change our thinking we can change our behavior. And we can. The foundations of our thoughts are the beliefs and values we have developed over time. These beliefs and values must be identified, reviewed and changed if we want to change our thought patterns and subsequent actions. -Mary Kurus

So how do we do it? It all begins with channeling our mentality. It all begins with slowing down our thought process. Frustration, anger, despair, and similar emotions move at a fast pace. As a matter of fact, research shows that whenever we feel angry or frustrated, there's a natural impulse that makes us want to attack immediately. That same research shows that the intensity of that impulse decreases after approximately ten seconds. That's why it is often recommended that we step back, breathe, and count to ten. In other words, it is often recommended that we slow down, stop our impulse, and choose the language that will guide us towards an action that will produce the most productive and positive results. Slow down. Then think differently. If we think it, then we can do it. We can embrace the struggle. We can get back up. We can dust it off. We can learn from it. And we can continue.

When I reflect on my childhood, I realize that I could have been another statistic, another case study. According to the article *"The Effects of Poverty on Children"* by Jeanne Brookks-Dunn, Ph.D and Greg J. Duncan, Ph.D, *"By and large, research supports the conclusion that family income has selective but, in some instances, quite substantial effects on child and adolescent well-being. Family income appears to be strongly related to children's ability and achievement. Children who live in extreme poverty or who live below the poverty line for multiple years appear, all other things being equal, to suffer the worst outcomes."* The answer they say is intervention at an early age. And that may be true. But I also feel that the intervention begins with the mental strength we need to overcome any obstacle. And the best way to develop that mental strength is through daily conditioning. Every day we must feed our minds with words and thoughts that make us feel empowered. And we cannot dismiss them as "just words" because there is a lot of power in those words. Don't strip them of their power. Give them their power. Give them their power every day. Every day, start your morning with a positive affirmation. If you can't think of one, do a quick Google search for "motivational words" and read one of those quotes as a way to start the day. Or bookmark pages in this book that you can read to yourself during breakfast. And then every day, end your evening with a list of at least 2-3 positive things that happened, whether it be something you did, something someone did for you, or something you saw or heard happen to someone else. Write that list as a text or email to yourself before you go to bed so that you can "sleep on positivity". Do it every day because when we feed ourselves these positive words and thoughts regularly, they give us a lot of power. Positive affirmations are the workout plan for the mind. And just like athletes exercise their bodies every day to be physically fit for every challenge, we must exercise our minds every day to be mentally fit for every challenge.

And according to the American Academy of Child and Adolescent Psychiatry, *"One in five adult Americans have lived with an alcoholic relative while growing up. In general, these children are at greater risk for having emotional problems than children whose parents are not alcoholics. Alcoholism runs in families, and children of alcoholics are four times more likely than other children to become alcoholics themselves."* Studies show that I could have been an anxious, depressed, substance abuser with low cognitive and verbal skills that potentially could have impeded my school performance, peer relationships, ability to develop and sustain intimate relationships, and performance on the job. I'm proud to say that I've risen above and beyond those trends and statistics. And it's not because I'm better than anybody else who has faced the same obstacles. I've just been able to discover my ability to stay positive and determined. And I remember the day I discovered my ability to be positive, though I didn't know it at the time. That next morning after hiding underneath the pillows of my mother's couch, I remember standing in the kitchen. And as I stood next to my mother, what I noticed…what I remember vividly…were my two aunts standing there…that was an important discovery…I had discovered that my mother and I had a supporting cast. And discovering that immediately after such a horrifying experience taught me the impact of following any negative

BEYOND LIMITATIONS

with a positive. For every negative that we are exposed to there is a positive we can expose ourselves to. And by doing that, we begin to associate those positives with those negatives. Notice what I've done: I took an unbelievably horrifying memory and turned it into a measure of how far I've come despite the odds. It's not about replacing the negative…my memory won't allow that. It's about attaching a positive. And that explains why people often say to me that I can find the positive in anything. As far as my ability to stay determined, I discovered while visiting my Aunt Grace that what we need is a desire to have. Compared to how my mother and I lived, my Aunt Grace was on cloud nine. She didn't live in a mansion. She didn't even live in a house. But her apartment building and her apartment to me, at such a young age, were majestic. And all I could think was if she and my mother grew up the same way and she achieved, then it's possible for me to achieve it too. And that's the second part of my ability to be determined: believing that it can and it will happen. And notice that my thought was that I could achieve it…I never thought in terms of my mother achieving that dream, nor Sonny achieving that dream…in my mind, I was the answer….if it is going to happen, I have to make it happen. And regardless of how hard I worked at school and worked to be a good kid, I knew that good fortune would not come tomorrow. So I would have to wait. And that's the last part of my ability to stay determined: patience. Determination is the result of a desire to have, a belief that it will happen, a willingness to hold yourself accountable, and the patience to wait. Start by clearly defining and visualizing what it is that you desire to have. Remind yourself daily.

The National Center for Victims of Crime states that *youth exposure to victimization is directly linked to negative outcomes for young people, including increased depression, substance abuse, risky sexual behavior, homelessness, and poor school performance. Youth victimization increases the odds of becoming a perpetrator of violent crimes, including felony assault and intimate partner violence, doubles the likelihood of problematic drug use, and increases the odds of committing property crimes.* The odds were against me. I beat the odds. We all can. We can all do anything. It's a mentality. And by no means do I want to imply that it is easy to beat the odds or that it is easy to adopt this mentality. And though it may be easier or even natural for some to have this mentality, it's possible for all of us to develop it. We've all beaten the odds; we've all overcome something, whether it was something big or small. Always keep those examples on the back burner of your mind so that memory can always be called upon when you face that next struggle. Overcoming the odds starts and progresses as a mentality.

Sonny was a presence in my life for many of my formative years, but for many of my significant years, I was an only child under the arms of a single mother. Trends show that I should have been doomed. Kathryn Wall reported in an article for News-Leader in 2012, *"Statistically, a child in a single-parent household is far more likely to experience violence, commit suicide, continue a cycle of poverty, become drug dependent, commit a crime or perform below his peers in education."* I escaped doom. It wasn't destiny. It was determination, something we all possess. Something we can all develop.

I realize that my story is unique to me. My struggles may have not been your struggles…maybe they're similar…maybe they are completely different….but regardless of what type of struggles, what type of obstacles, what type of challenges we have faced, we face now, or we will face down the road, the road to a higher ground is within our reach. Truth be told, I don't have to fully understand what you're "going through" to know that you can "get through".

The key is how badly you "want" to get through.

BEYOND LIMITATIONS

RISE BEYOND

If you want to rise beyond, change your perception of the struggle and see it as the challenge that is going to make you stronger to get to where you want to go. Elevate Your Mind.

If you want to rise beyond, choose to view the life you don't want to live, as the life you "fear" to continue living. Many resist using the word "fear" because they don't want to be perceived by others or by themselves as cowards. But I'm not talking about "fear" in terms of "cowardice". I'm talking "fear" in terms "drive". Rewire the Fear. Embrace the Struggle. Empower Yourself.

If you want to rise beyond, choose to do it, not only for yourself, but also for someone else whose life you want to change. I'm inspired by an artist like Will.i.am who said that he bought his mother a house before he bought himself a house; he bought his mother a car before he bought himself a car. For me, it was never a matter of not doing something so that I don't disappoint someone like my mother. It was a matter of doing something so that I could give to or provide for my mother. And now it's a matter of doing something for my wife and my children. Do It For Yourself. Do It For Them.

If you want to rise beyond, you have to step up and do it. Otherwise you have to question whether or not you really want it. No excuses, no one to blame, no hopes that someone else will do it for you. Choose What You Want. Confirm Your Commitment.

If you want to rise beyond, get involved in as much as you can. Do many different things. Rest when you can, but don't be idle for too long. Keep Your Self Active. Keep Yourself Busy. Keep Yourself Going.

BEYOND LIMITATIONS

If you want to rise beyond, do more than you are expected to do. Notice that I don't just promote rising above; I'm about rising beyond where we want to go. Never Settle. Go Beyond Expectations.

If you want to rise beyond, get a mentor and take direction from others who are trying to help you. Surround yourself with people who are motivated to see you prosper, progress, and succeed. There are people in your life who want to see you make it. Follow your guides. Follow their lead. And I feel the need to add this: the people who gave me direction in my life did two things that are absolutely necessary for all of us to excel: they emphasized the importance of education and they emphasized the importance of exposure to a world outside of what was familiar.

If you want to rise beyond, choose your language. What you say, how you act, what you read, and what you listen to has an impact on your mood and your performance. Talk Positive. Talk Success.

In closing, everyone struggles. They say that the most successful people fail more than anyone else. That's because they never give up. They keep trying. It's a mentality.

It starts and progresses as a mentality.

In his book *$1000 and an Idea*, Sam Wyly wrote, after remembering the words of Winston Churchill who urged the British to "never give in, never" despite the nightly bombings of the Nazis', "The thing is that winning requires hard work, clear thinking and not losing requires exactly the same; and neither has anything to do with becoming a hero or a quitter. Sometimes, though, both have to do with being stubborn, and being stubborn when running into a brick wall has more than once been bruising." And Wyly summarizes, "Never mistake a single battle for the whole war."

Success is a process that contains plenty of struggles and the struggles are instrumental steps towards your desired goal.

BEYOND LIMITATIONS

We all struggle with something. And the worst part about any struggle we face is that struggles have the power to wear away at our drive and motivation. Sometimes we feel so defeated that we want to quit. We wonder why we're being punished. Why are we so unlucky? But that's when we have to dig deepest and find that inner strength to keep fighting. Because struggle is not about being unlucky or being punished. It's about developing a strength that will build the fire from the ashes.

All I ever want to do every day I wake up is build a fire from the ashes. I want to help myself, help my family, my friends, my students, and anyone else within my proverbial reach to rise above any struggle we may face and soar beyond the limits that do not exist. We all have dreams. We can all live them.

"It's natural. We dream every night. So we have to dream every day. But unlike those dreams that appear while we sleep and disappear when we wake up, the real dreams, let's call them our aspirations and goals, never disappear unless your desire and drive to achieve disappears. Keep dreaming. Keep driving to make it happen." - Marc Williams

"One of the most difficult things everyone has to learn is that for your entire life you must keep fighting and adjusting if you hope to survive. No matter who you are or what your position is you must keep fighting for whatever it is you desire to achieve." -George Allen

Never stop fighting.
Never stop until you RISE BEYOND your limitations!